An Architectural History *of the* South Carolina College, *1801-1855*

Published in Columbia, South Carolina, during the
one hundred and seventy-fifth anniversary of the establishment
of the University of South Carolina
and the two-hundredth anniversary
of the establishment of the
United States of America.

Robert Mills's proposal for the South Carolina College. From the collection of the South Carolina Department of Archives and History.

DORCHESTER COUNTY LIBRARY
3 0018 000513669

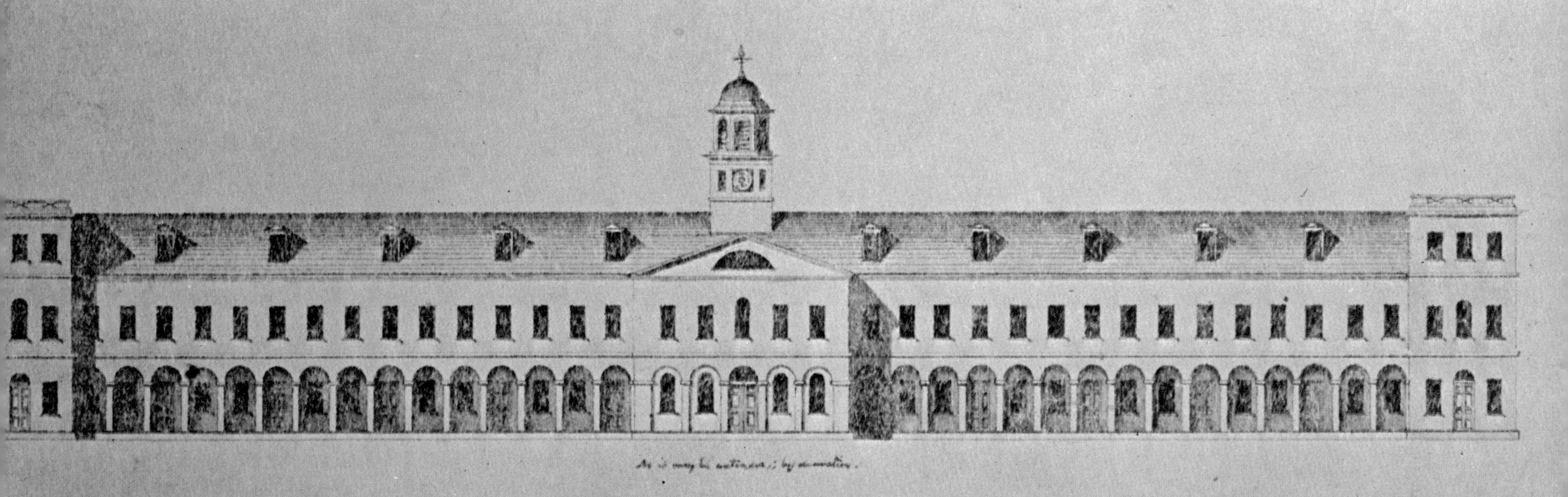
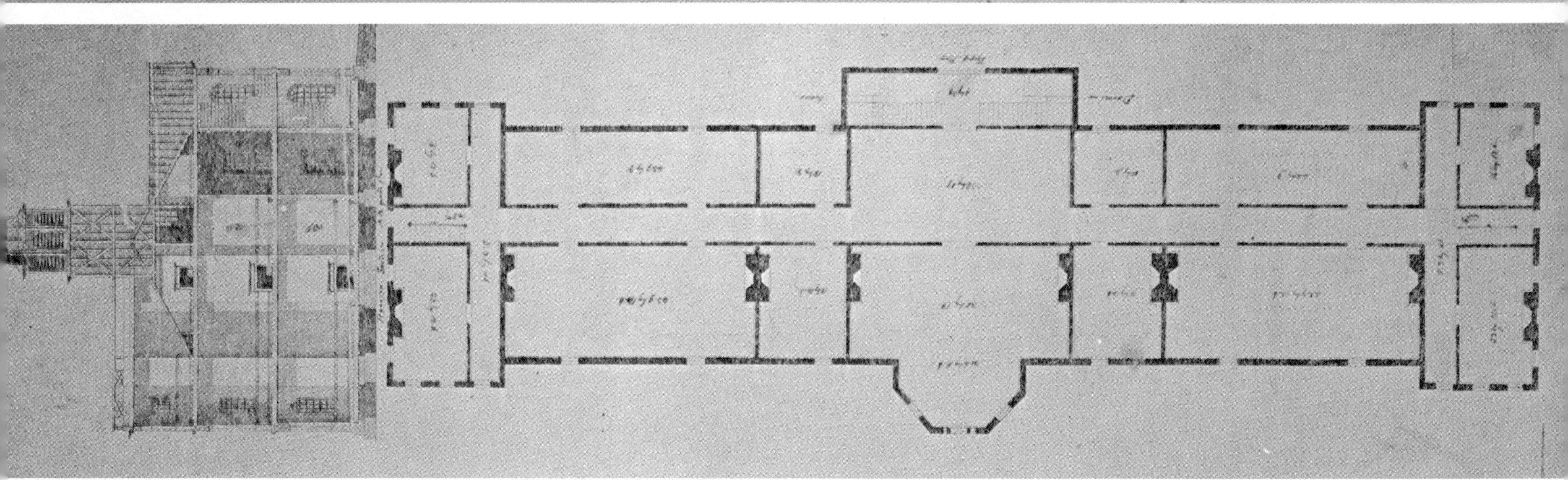

PHOTOGRAPH: Charles Gay

The north side of what is now called "The Horseshoe," painted around 1850 by William Harrison Scarborough (1812–1871). From the Collection of the South Caroliniana Library.

PHOTOGRAPH: Charles Gay

The south side of "The Horseshoe," painted around 1850 by William Harrison Scarborough. From the collection of the South Caroliniana Library.

AROLINIANA LIBRARY

Opposite
Photograph: Kathleen Lewis Sloan

The South Caroliniana Library in May, 1968. The building is usually referred to as "Caroliniana."

Photograph: Kathleen Lewis Sloan

Rear view of "Caroliniana," showing the semicircular outer wall of the stairwell. The garden in which this photograph was taken in May, 1968, is a quiet and lovely corner of the campus.

PHOTOGRAPH: Kathleen Lewis Sloan

"The Horseshoe" photographed from the south side in April, 1976, looking toward Sumter Street.

Photograph: Kathleen Lewis Sloan

"The Horseshoe" photographed from the north side in April, 1976, looking toward Sumter Street. The Maxcy Monument is on the left.

Photograph: Kathleen Lewis Sloan
Rear view of the President's House in August, 1976, showing the chimney pots that were designed so that rain would not come down the chimneys.

Opposite
Photograph: Kathleen Lewis Sloan
The President's House in April, 1976.

PHOTOGRAPH: Kathleen Lewis Sloan

DeSaussure College (East Wing). This photograph was taken in August, 1976, to record the restoration of the building that was then under way.

Opposite
PHOTOGRAPH: Kathleen Lewis Sloan

DeSaussure College, August, 1976. This view silhouettes the roofline of the central core of the building from the northeast corner. The "tree" on the left is a watermelon crepe myrtle.

An Architectural History *of the* SOUTH CAROLINA COLLEGE 1801-1855

by

John Morrill Bryan

With a Foreword by Paul F. Norton

UNIVERSITY OF SOUTH CAROLINA PRESS, COLUMBIA, SOUTH CAROLINA

Published in Columbia, S.C., by the
University of South Carolina Press, 1976

First Printing, 1976 (*hardcover, boxed, limited to 200 copies*)
Second Printing, 1976 (*paperback*)

Manufactured in the United States of America
DESIGNED BY *Larry Hirst*

Frontispiece PHOTOGRAPH: Kathleen Lewis Sloan
These workmen were restoring Elliott College when they stopped for lunch one day in August, 1976.

Library of Congress Cataloging in Publication Data

Bryan, John Morrill.
An architectural history of the South Carolina College, 1801–1855.
Bibliography: p.
Includes index.
1. South Carolina. University—Buildings. I. Title.
LD5034.6.B79 378.757'71 76-54242
ISBN 0-87249-351-2
ISBN 0-87249-352-0 pbk.

for Martha Scoville Bryan, Charles Scoville Bryan, *and* Mary Morrill Bryan

Foreword

The history of architecture, like most humanistic studies, has developed over the past two centuries in numerous directions. It includes writings on the carpenter's lowly nail and the stone mason's chisel marks, lofty essays on the rib vaulting of cathedrals and the ultimate meaning of a Greek column, and books devoted to all types of buildings in almost every country in the world. But this is not all, for the architects themselves have had biographers, and Ruskin, with a host of followers, introduced architecture as a field for aesthetic criticism. In short, architecture, the great social art, has been regarded, like literature, as a vast panoply open to the view of art lovers and to the study of scholars, as well as serving the very practical purposes of which we are all aware.

John Bryan's carefully conducted research has resulted in a book which combines all the above points of view concerning architecture, as he skillfully interwove knowledge of the building trades, early town-planning, deliberations of building committees, and so on. For instance, his scrutiny of building agreements and specifications has revealed a method of exterior wall-finishing calling for the "painting and penciling" of brick, found elsewhere, but apparently common in Columbia, S.C.; and he surprisingly discovered the influence of New England building practice in the use of what he calls "the Boston Granite Style." The building techniques used in South Carolina are recognized as important in characterizing the provincial architectural style, but Bryan takes a larger view by making comparisons in both plans and style with earlier college buildings in the North. He proves the validity of the relationships by showing many direct connections of the early South Carolina buildings with their distinguished counterparts at Yale, Princeton, Dartmouth, etc. Not only were these college buildings visually similar, but they also provided very similar interior spaces, for the educational activities promoted within were themselves alike.

Most people are inclined to think of South Carolina in the early nineteenth century as a rather backward, undeveloped country without much real need for a college of distinction, but from the very beginning, Bryan points out, the College was intended to take the lead in providing the best possible education in a variety of fields for the young men of the state. Witness the purchase all at once of a complete library of 5,000 volumes from London booksellers, and more important architecturally, the continuing attempts to select the best available architects to plan the buildings. Robert Mills, one of the few great architects of the earlier nineteenth century, submitted plans and gave advice at numerous times; Peter Banner, highly respected in New England, was in the competition for the very first building; and Benjamin Henry Latrobe (shortly to be appointed architect of the Capitol in Washington) wrote a letter making valuable suggestions. Unfortunately, a few local builder-architects were hired whose designs were less than creative. Bryan, by uncovering the names and backgrounds of all these architects enriches his study immensely. He also directly demonstrates how sincere the governor, the legislators, the trustees and the professors all were in their concerted actions at gaining recognition for the fledgling college and in guaranteeing for future generations, insofar as they were able, an institution of higher education of which they could be justly proud. What delight all those connected in any way with the College must have felt when Professor M. J. Williams, after much toil and frustration, installed a new large astronomical telescope, in an observatory specially constructed for it, could tell President James Thornwell that the telescope "fully answers the expectations I had formed of its power and finish."

As with all attempts at comprehensive,detailed research, Bryan has not found every answer to the questions he poses. But this is owing to the loss of written documents and architectural drawings, not to any lack of persistence on the part of the author. In fact, the reader perusing these pages will be struck by the large number of letters and documents, quoted frequently in full, which have survived various fires and the ravages of recalcitrant students who were not always in sympathy with the ideals of the institution. It is highly unlikely that anyone can ever add much of importance to the knowledge gathered herein.

There are many published studies on the architecture of specific colleges and universities throughout the country. However, to my knowledge, none succeeds so well as this in combining in the broadest and best sense all the aspects of college life, of architectural planning and style, economy, human despair, and the joys of hard-earned accomplishment.

Paul F. Norton
University of Massachusetts
Amherst
6 September 1976

Preface and Acknowledgments

> The greatest glory of a building is not in its stones, nor in its gold. Its glory is in its Age, and in that deep sense of voicefulness, of stern watching, of mysterious sympathy, nay, even of approval or condemnation, which we feel in walls that have long been washed by the passing waves of humanity.[1]
>
> John Ruskin, *The Seven Lamps of Architecture*

Without any fanfare work began on the initial buildings of the South Carolina College in the spring of 1802. During the next half century the College grew, and in 1855 twelve buildings defined the College grounds—the area that is known today as the "horseshoe." This cluster of classrooms, dormitories, faculty residences, and library facilities is recognized as a notable example of collegiate architectural development in America. In 1970 the significance of the old campus prompted the United States Department of the Interior to add the buildings and grounds to the National Register of Historic Sites. Our epigraph articulates the evocative effect of this setting, for while lingering here we find that images form in the mind's eye of Professor William Ellet in 1840 in the sun behind the south range with his new daguerreotype apparatus, or Francis Lieber writing the famous *Legal and Political Hermeneutics* in the quiet study which he described as being "a spot somewhat sacred to me," upstairs in the building that now bears his name. Then too, there are the more sinister associations. The stillness which pervades the dignified reading room of the South Caroliniana Library recalls the calamity which Thomas Park, Librarian and Treasurer of the College, conveyed to the Trustees in his letter of 25 November 1840:

> It has become my painful duty to acquaint your Honorable Body of one of the most disastrous occurrances that ever happened to me. On the third night of the present session of the college, there was stolen from me the sum of $2600.[2]

Under the cover of darkness an unseen hand had forced the lower drawer of the librarian's desk and had stolen the tuition monies for the fall term.

Even the tranquil green itself evokes the obstreperous ebullience that is always a part of student life. A memorable evening on the green, for example, is presented in a letter which William C. Preston, President of the College, wrote to Governor Seabrook in 1850:

[1] John Ruskin, *The Seven Lamps of Architecture* (London: George Allen, Sunnyside, Orpington, 1897), 339.

[2] Among the manuscript records of the South Carolina College in the collections of the South Carolina Department of Archives and History (cited henceforth as SCAH).

> We had hardly adjourned from a faculty meeting before I saw unequivocal indications of an approaching commotion. At twilight noises began to arise in the Campus, and large groups to be formed before the Professors' houses. In a short time the mob increased to a multitude. Shouts and riotous yells were heard; and as darkness closed a bright flame arose from the midst of the crowd. Upon hastening to the spot with some of the Professors, I witnessed a scene of confusion, uproar and turbulence, beyond what I had ever seen. There was a general confusion of clamorous voices, directed to no particular subject. The whole College apparently was assembled—very many drunk, all frantic; no marked prevalence of evil passion, though a prodigious display of tumultuary excitement—one boy was brandishing a sword, but with no indication of murderous intent—though its flashing in the light of the blazing fire looked fearful enough. The fire was consuming a table covered with a pile of Books—the Chemical Text Books, which the members of the Junior Class has devoted as a solemn sacrifice to the flames.[3]

Anecdotes (the Roach-Adams duel of 1833 comes to mind, in which a student was killed following an argument in the Steward's Hall over a platter of food) must not divert us from our primary concern which is the history of the buildings themselves. The principal significance of these structures does not lie in accrued associations. Instead, stylistic characteristics, techniques of construction, the very fabric of the buildings themselves and the documents that record their genesis, these are the things that make the College buildings serve us as a mirror of their age. Architecture results from the confluence of many forces, and the designer of buildings must respond to constraints which do not impinge upon the other arts. The painter and the sculptor enjoy a wide margin for idiosyncrasy, but the architect must chart a course that reflects utility, economy, and stability as well as taste. As a result of these parameters, the College buildings make concrete many aspects of life in early nineteenth-century South Carolina.

An examination of these buildings is aided by the survival of a remarkable collection of memoranda, contracts, drawings, and miscellaneous emphemera. As narrative, most of these materials leave much to be desired. Nevertheless, they are quoted here at length, for through these documents the builders speak for themselves. Using these records we can substantiate a number of events which shed new light upon the antebellum cultural milieu in the upcountry of South Carolina. The submissions in the initial design competition of 1801, for instance, exemplify the transfer of architectural style from New England and the middle Atlantic states into Charleston, and from Charleston we see how motifs filtered into the hinterland. The deliberations of the Trustees after the contest demonstrate local notions about the interrelationships of topography and health. Here we also learn something about the intended social structure of the College and gain insight into the growth of the City of Columbia. The records of the designers and contractors of these buildings are of great interest. Studying the architectural history of the College, we discover a great deal about the career of Robert Mills. We can demonstrate that his earliest known design was a submission in the College contest. Then we can show that Mills, after sharing the competition award with Richard Clark, sent to Governor Drayton several "elegant" elevations of the building plans adopted by the Board of Trustees. These drawings determined the character of the facades of Rutledge and DeSaussure Colleges. Robert Mills continued to work for the College. Investigating his design for the Maxcy Monument, we discover the seeds of his masterpiece—the Washington Monument in the nation's capital. The most notable discovery concerning Robert

[3] In the Miscellaneous File of the manuscript records relating to the history of the College in the collections of the South Caroliniana Library (cited henceforth as SCL).

Mills is found in the presentation of his schematic drawings for the South Caroliniana Library, the first free-standing academic library in the United States.

None of this material would have been unearthed now had it not been for the support of many individuals and organizations. For me this disinterested cooperation has been the most heartening aspect of the project. The commitment of Dr. William H. Patterson, President of the University of South Carolina, to the historic character of the College provided the impetus for this book. The research was undertaken as part of the restoration of the College buildings, a project which President Patterson initiated as the contribution of the University to the observance of the Bicentennial. The University Provost, Keith E. Davis, and the Vice President of Operations, Harold Brunton, have provided support for my work. A generous grant from the Research and Productive Scholarship Committee of the University has facilitated the necessary travel and has aided in the acquisition of illustrative materials. Many librarians, archivists, and curators have been of great assistance. Mr. E. L. Inabinett, Librarian, and Mr. Allen H. Stokes, Manuscripts Librarian, of the South Caroliniana Library have buoyed me up as I waded through the manuscript records of the College. Mr. Charles E. Lee, Director of the South Carolina Department of Archives and History, and Miss Wylma Wates and the Search Room staff of the Archives, and the late Miss Helen G. McCormack of the South Carolina Historical Society, have helped me to locate materials related to the history of the state. Beyond South Carolina, I am particularly grateful for the courteous professionalism of Mr. Jack Jackson and Mr. Donald C. Kelley of the Boston Athenaeum, Mr. James Goode of the Smithsonian Institution, Mr. Ford Peatross of the Library of Congress, and the staff of the Avery Library of Columbia University.

I owe a singular debt of gratitude to Stanley A. South of the Institute of Archeology and Anthropology of South Carolina, for early in the project his excavations on the College grounds revealed several points of interest. Exemplary archival spadework was done by Janet C. Lee, then a student at the University. Another student, Miss Beverley H. Means, has been an ideal editorial assistant and typist. All of these people played a formative role in the making of this book. It is regrettable that I am not able to single out each of those points at which one of their suggestions served as a catalyst and caused a motley assortment of facts to coalesce into a constellation. In this regard, as the work progressed I derived particular benefit and pleasure from my conversations with Dr. Walter B. Edgar, Assistant Professor of History at the University, and Miss Anna Wells Rutledge and Mr. Albert Simons of Charleston. Mr. John Califf, architect, more than anyone else, often forced me to go back to the drawing board; I am especially grateful to him, for his participation consistently typified the most urbane and rewarding aspect of the work. He was the runner-up for the dedication.

J. M. B.
4 July 1976

Contents

List of Illustrations

A NOTE ON PRONUNCIATIONS

In South Carolina the following pronunciations have been preferred for approximately 200 years:

DeSaussure—DESSasor
Huger—yooJEE
Legare—leGREE

The names are derived from Huguenot French refugees whose descendants had been thoroughly assimilated into the English-speaking population by the time of the Revolution.

An Architectural History *of the* South Carolina College, *1801-1855*

The Design Competition

Robert Mills, Richard Clark, Benjamin Henry Latrobe, Peter Banner, et al.

1801-1802

On 10 July 1793, John Drayton (1767–1822) of Charleston, South Carolina, wrote an essay entitled "An account of the public Schools at Boston. A descant upon the blessings which attend patriotism and religion when rightly enjoyed. A contrast between the state of information possessed by the inhabitants of the commonwealth of Massachusetts, and those of S. Carolina."

Here he noted the benefits of public education in Boston saying that through their schools "their youth are trained up to industry, and social affection: and are persuaded that when they grow up, they will never forget those early obligations, received from the fostering hands of their country. Sweet school for every public virtue! —It was thus, that Greece sowed those seeds of patriotism, which long made her shine unrivalled, in the history of nations."[1] This enthusiastic endorsement of the social and political benefits of education is later echoed in his proposal to establish the South Carolina College. In 1800 and then again in 1801, Drayton, as Governor of South Carolina, proposed the creation of a centrally located, state supported college.

Speaking to the legislature, he proclaimed that through the creation of a central state college "The friendships of young men would thence be promoted and strengthened throughout the State, and our political union be much advanced thereby."[2] His proposal met with success, and on 19 December 1801, he signed "An Act to Establish a College at Columbia."

On 4 November 1801, the Board of Trustees was convened in a meeting which initiated the development of the South Carolina College. The minutes of this meeting record that Governor Drayton was elected President of the Board of Trustees, that a committee was established "to draw up Rules, for preserving Order and Decorum at the Meetings, and during the deliberations, of the Board of Trustees, and, that the said Committee be also charged with the further Duty, of determining on some Appropriate Device, for

[1] John Drayton, *Letters Written During a Tour through the Northern and Eastern States of America* (Charleston: Harrison and Bowen, 1794), 53.

[2] Edwin L. Green, *A History of the University of South Carolina* (Columbia: The State, 1916), 11. Daniel Walker Hollis, *University of South Carolina*, Volume I, *South Carolina College* (Columbia: University of South Carolina Press, 1951), 3–21, presents a sweeping view of the forces which led to the creation of the College.

the Common Seal of the said College." The Board also resolved

that Col. Taylor, Col. Hampton, Rev. Mr. Dunlap, the Honorable Judge Brevard, John Chesnut, Henry D. Ward, Bartlee Smythe, and James B. Richardson Esquires, or a majority of them, be a Committee to examine and report at the next meeting a proper site whereon to erect the College at Columbia; and to enquire into the practicability of procuring stone, and to suggest the most economical means of procuring the same, for the use of the College, and to offer by advertisement a premium not exceeding One Hundred Dollars for the discovery of Stone proper for the use of said building.

On motion Resolved that his Excellency the Governor, President of this Board, do cause an advertizement to be made inviting artists to prepare and transmit to him under seal, on or before the fourth Monday in May next, original Plans suitable for the erection of a College capable of accommodating the greatest possible number of Students; besides having a sufficient number of Public rooms adapted to the exercises of the institution, and, for the accommodation of the Professors. The Expences of carrying the said plan in Execution, not to exceed Fifty Thousand Dollars, and that the President of this Board, do offer a premium of three hundred dollars for the best original plan for the erection of the said College, which shall be transmitted to him, on or before the Day above said; and which on examination shall be approved of and accepted by the Board of Trustees.

The President of this Board also had in charge from the Board, to request of the Presidents of Colleges in the United States, a Description or plan, of the College over which they Preside, and it was further determined, that the two above mentioned premiums, as well as any expence attending the obtaining descriptions or plans, from the Presidents of Colleges, be paid out of the appropriation for Building the College.

The Board, was then adjourned to the fourth Monday in May next, then to meet at His Excellency the Governor's in the City of Charleston, precisely at ten O'Clock in the forenoon.

Had we been standing outside the Charleston home of Governor Drayton that morning in 1801, we would have seen the Trustees departing. Among them, we would have noticed particularly Col. Thomas Taylor (1743–1833) and Col. Wade Hampton (1752–1835).[3] Contemporaneous sources tell us that Col. Taylor, then fifty-seven years of age, presented a commanding figure; six feet, two inches tall, he possessed a military bearing and assurance that suggested his prominence in civic affairs. He had participated in the first and second Provincial Congresses; he had seen extensive military action, had borne responsibility under fire during the revolutionary battles of Fort Cary, Fishing Creek and Fish Dam Ford, Blackstock, Fort Granby and Wright's Bluff, Fort Motte and Quinby Bridge. He and Wade Hampton had served together under General Thomas Sumter. Hampton's meritorious action at Eutaw Springs had made him famous throughout the state.

In 1801, Hampton's new enterprise—the cultivation of cotton in the upcountry—was much discussed. It was considered to be promising, for his yield in 1799 was some 600 bales and was worth approximately ninety thousand dollars. Hampton and Taylor had known each other for many years. Their mutual fortunes had been for a decade bound up in the growth and development of Columbia, the state capital since 1786. It is interesting to note that these two men had purchased as a joint venture in 1785 some 18,500 acres of land along the Congaree River for ten cents an acre. Subsequently, it was from Col. Thomas Taylor and his brother John that the state acquired two square miles near the Hampton-Taylor purchase for the site of the capital. Col. Thomas Taylor served on the state commission which surveyed and divided this land into streets, blocks and lots. Many of these lots were purchased by Wade Hampton, then the wealthiest man in Richland County. It is un-

[3] For biographical notes concerning Taylor, see B. F. Taylor, "Col. Thomas Taylor," *The South Carolina Historical and Genealogical Magazine*, XVII (October, 1926), 204–11.

derstandable that these two men were appointed to the committee of the Board which sought a location for the new college. One imagines them together on the cobbled walk, discussing the proper setting for the new college, the tall and stately Taylor, and Hampton, whom a diarist described saying:

> Colonel H's personal appearance is not very striking. Stature not over middling. Dresses in good clothes, but has nothing showy about him. A great enemy to finery, and treats it with marked contempt. There is nothing commanding or peculiarly dignified in his appearance; though he has an easy and becoming dignity of manners. He appears to much the best advantage when mounted; being an unusually expert horseman. When standing, and especially if engaged in conversation, he is very apt to rest on one leg, and to throw out the other so far as to give him a stooping posture; while at the same time his arms are placed akimbo, and his eyes cast on the ground.[4]

Three months passed before the site committee made its recommendation to the Board at the meeting of 24 May 1801. Although there are no records of the deliberations of this committee, we can reconstruct with some confidence several factors which must have influenced their report through a review of maps, census data, engravings and contemporaneous diaries. The Act establishing the College made it plain that the institution was to be located in Columbia, within that area sold by the Taylors and defined by the survey of 1786 (Figure 1). The Act stipulated that the "Trustees, with the concurrence of the Commissioners of Columbia, shall be empowered to make choice of any square or squares, yet unsold, in the town of Columbia, for the purpose of erecting said College, and the buildings attached thereto, having a strict reference to every advantage and convenience necessary for such institution."

[4] Edward Hooker, *Diary of Edward Hooker, 1805–1808* (Washington: Government Printing Office, 1897), 850.

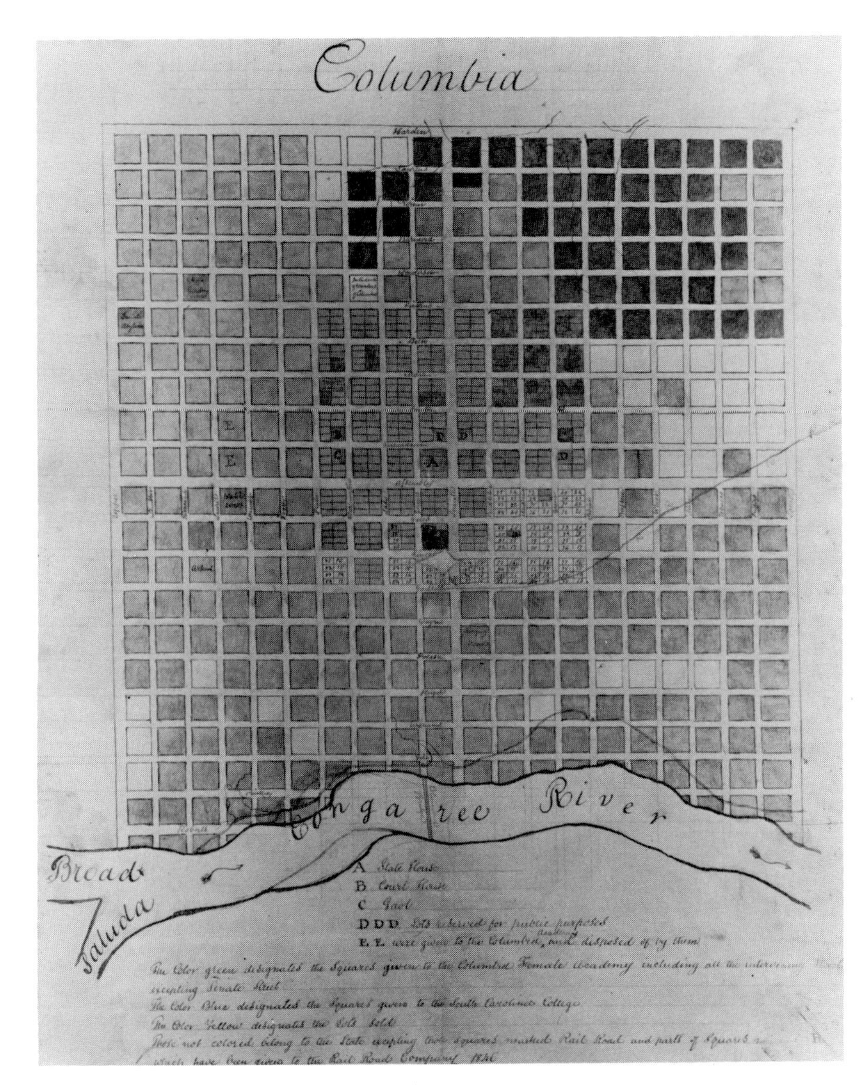

FIGURE 1. Survey of the City of Columbia, South Carolina, by J. G. Guignard, 1786, from the collection of the South Carolina Department of Archives and History.

For an understanding of the subsequent architectural development of the College, it is important to note that the reference to the city squares presupposed a rectilinear ground plan related to the grid of the city streets. We may also assume that the language within the act making "reference to every advantage and convenience necessary to such an institution" connotes contemporary beliefs about the interrelationship of topography and health. When later we consider the origins of the earliest College buildings we will have occasion to review the impact of the street pattern upon the ground plan. Here, however, dealing with the location of the campus, we might recall that since the first century before Christ when the Roman writer Vitruvius had codified classical building practice in his *Ten Books on Architecture*, it had been widely held that "First comes the choice of a very healthy site. Such a site will be high . . . without marshes in the neighborhood: For when the morning breezes blow . . . if they bring with them mists from marshes and, mingled with the mist, the poisonous breath of the creatures of the marshes to be wafted into the bodies of the inhabitants, they will make the site unhealthy."[5]

Vitruvius goes on to say that "the next step is the apportionment of house lots . . . and the laying out of streets and alleys with regard to climatic conditions. They will be properly laid out if foresight is employed to exclude the winds from the alleys. Cold winds are disagreeable, hot winds enervating, moist winds unhealthy."[6]

In seeking a site for the College, the Trustees may have recalled the debates in the House of Representatives concerning the selection of a site for Columbia itself. In the House on 14 March 1786, Patrick Calhoun had spoken effectively against the "unwholesome" marshy region of Santee proposed by General Sumter. Calhoun's advocacy of the high ground adjacent to "Friday's Ferry" carried the day. During the debate, Dr. John Budd of Charleston suggested that the Act establishing the capital should stipulate streets at least sixty feet wide, as this was necessary to good health in warm climates. His suggestion, like Calhoun's, was adopted.

In its settlement pattern as well as in its site, Columbia followed Vitruvian criteria, for the crest of the plateau, the most desirable land, was developed first. To comprehend this, we must keep in mind that the Guignard Survey is a conceptual document; it does not depict the cityscape of 1790, nor 1800, nor even of 1810. This initial map includes streets which were not actually in use until long after the College had been established. To envision the community as it existed in the spring of 1801 during the deliberations of the College Site Selection Committee we may review the observations of Governor Drayton, Edward Hooker, or travelogues such as the *Emigrant's Directory* and Michaux's *Travels*.

Drayton, in his *View of South Carolina*, written in 1802, describes Columbia:

> Columbia is the seat of government of this state; and its situation is just below the confluence of Broad and Saluda rivers on the eastern side of the Congaree river. It was so called by act of assembly in 1786; at which time measures were taken for the first settling of the town: and the departments of government met there in December, 1789; and continue to do so at stated periods. This town is laid off by a regular plan; its streets intersecting each other at right angles. The buildings are erected about three quarters of a mile from the Congaree, on a ridge of high land, near three hundred feet above the level of that river; from which a delightful prospect is presented. Here the state-house, situated on a beautiful eminence, is to be seen, at the distance of many miles, from various parts of the country. And soon, we hope, the South-Carolina College will rise an ornament to the town; respectable from its establishment; but still more from the learning and

[5] Vitruvius, *The Ten Books on Architecture*, trans. Morris Hicky Morgan (New York: Dover, 1960), 17.
[6] Ibid., 24–25.

friendship, which a national institution, like this, cannot fail to promote among the youth from all parts of the state; an object, particularly desirable to all true lovers of their country. Some successful attempts have been made, at Columbia, in raising grapes and making wine; and a few casks of this grateful liquor have been there made by Mr. Benjamin Waring; whose flavor was agreeable, and not unlike Sicily wine.[7]

Edward Hooker (1785–1846) arrived in Columbia on 4 November 1805 and recorded his impression of the city:

Monday Nov. 11th. The township of Columbia is not large; being only two miles square. This territory is laid out into lots and streets; but not more than one third of the streets are yet opened; and of those which are opened, several have not more than two or three buildings upon them. The State House is placed on an eminence directly in the center of the township, though very far from the center of the buildings. The principal street is Richardson Street which runs on the east side of the State House: although State Street which runs on the west side was designed, by the commissioners who planned the town, for the principal one. State Street is the central one: and the State House, though made with two fronts, was however constructed as to present its handsomest front to the west. Yet public choice has so far disregarded the original plan that State Street is, even to this time, to a considerable extent, overrun with bushes. That part of the town which is not put into open streets is, for the most part, a wilderness of pines. Now and then is seen a cultivated spot of a few acres which forms an exception. The State House is very large on the ground, but yet so low as to be entirely void of anything like just proportion. It has only two stories; and one of these is partly below the natural surface of the ground, and is of brick plaistered over. The lower story is appropriated to the Treasurer's, Secretary's, and Surveyor General's offices. There are several other rooms, which, as far as I can learn, are used for little else than lodging rooms for the goats that run loose about the streets, and which, as the doors are never shut, have at all times free access. The court house is a much handsomer building—of brick, two stories high. There is only one church in the town. The people think it "a very neat, pretty building"; but I am certain there is not a country parish in Connecticut but would disdain not to build a better one, in case they were about to build at all. It is not more than one third as large as Framington Church; has no steeple; and the inside is in a very coarse and unfinished state. It is not plaistered—and the seats are merely movable benches placed promiscuously on the floor. The pulpit and altar are finished and present a neat enough appearance. The same is true of the outside. —The houses generally are built of wood and many of them, though small, are pretty. These peculiarities distinguish them from Connecticut houses: They are generally narrower —having for the convenience of ventilation, only one tier of rooms. They are without cellars; being set up on blocks or stones considerably above the ground, and left open below the floors: —it being an opinion somewhat prevalent that cellars are unhealthy. They are unconnected with the kitchens. The chimneys are built and carried up, all the way on the outside of the house. —The execution of all the work that I have noticed seems to me very different from that of Connecticut. Everything has a shackling, flimsy look—Joints are parting—Boards are coming off—Plaistering is full of cracks and breaks.

The number of houses and stores in the town I should judge to be over an hundred. —The inhabitants have no special privileges at present except a power of making regulations concerning the streets, public wells and market, through the agency of a committee who are stiled "Commissioners of the Streets." They are however expecting ere long to get from the legislature a charter of incorporation, which shall confer upon them the same powers with Camden and other little cities or boroughs.

Richardson Street and some others are lined, in part, with a beautiful tree called the Pride of India. In some few places a native pine is left standing, though they are every day diminishing in number. The inhabitants do not like them at all; and will not for a moment admit the idea that so cheap a tree as the pine which overruns their whole state can possibly contribute to the embellishment of a town. Hence they have commenced against them a "war of extermination". Around the

[7] John Drayton, *A View of South Carolina as Respects Her Natural and Civil Concerns* (Charleston: W. P. Yong, 1802), 211–12.

State House are left standing some lofty forest oaks which afford a grateful shade, and give the scenery a rural and a charming cast.[8]

Edward Hooker drew a map (Figure 2) to accompany this passage. We note that only 21 of the projected 380 city blocks were extant and that the initial settlement lay centered north and south along Richardson Street, now called Main Street, following the crest of the plateau above the river. In an entry of 22 March 1808, Hooker was more specific about the settlement patterns:

> * * * At 4 o'clock rode out with Brother J. and returning we agreed to reckon up the number of dwelling houses in Columbia; —calling those dwelling houses which families reside in or designed for such use. So we rode through Richardson and two or three other streets and counted them. The result was one hundred and twelve: viz on Richardson or the Main street 52. On the different streets east of Main street 46. On the streets west, or between the Main street and river 19. I suppose about five or six new ones are building which we did not count. * * * [9]

With this information we can envision the setting reviewed by the men seeking a location for the South Carolina College. Columbia was a settlement of some one hundred frame dwellings, one church, two government buildings and unpaved streets. It was not impressive. If the town made a favorable impression, it must have been due to what Hooker has termed its "rural" and "charming cast." On this point books such as Michaux's *Travels* and the *Emigrant's Directory* have left us commentaries corroborating Edward Hooker's *Diary*. Both of these, for example, refer to the characteristic yellow and grey trim of Columbia's houses, praising them modestly for their "very respectable appearance."[10]

Despite the simple character of the new capital, its city plan evinced a sense of purpose and held out a promise for the future. To insure the development of an architectural setting worthy of the new capital, the legislature had required each purchaser of land within the city "to build thereon a frame, wood, stone, or brick house, not less than thirty feet long and eighteen feet in the clear, with brick or stone chimneys, within the space of three years from the time of such purchase." It had also established two boulevards, "two principal streets, running through the centre of the town at right angles, of one hundred and fifty feet wide; which said land shall be, and the same is hereby declared to be, vested in the said commissioners, and their lawful successors, for the use of this State." Furthermore, it had retained eight acres "for the purpose of erecting such public buildings as may be necessary and as shall be most convenient and ornamental."[11]

The original plan of Columbia has often been praised, but an objective reappraisal reveals many shortcomings, liabilities which impinged upon the location of the new college. The Guignard Survey was predicated upon a rectilinear grid. Regularity is the principal asset of such a city plan. Its liabilities, however, include a total disregard for distinctive topographical features, a failure to create and emphasize civic nodal points and an inability to accommodate diagonal traffic. The inappropriateness of the grid for the Columbia site is evidenced by the fact that the city did not develop along the major axes—Senate and Assembly streets—envisioned by its founders. Assembly Street, the proposed north-south axial boulevard, was simply poorly conceived at the outset. Traversing pre-

[8] Hooker, *Diary*, 853–55.

[9] Ibid., 911.

[10] F. A. Michaux, *Travels to the West of the Alleghany Mountains, in the States of Ohio, Kentucky, and Tennessea, and Back to Charleston, by the Upper Carolines* (London: D. N. Shury, 1805), 272–73, and the anonymous *Geographical, Historical, Commercial and Agricultural View of the United States of America; Forming a Complete Emigrant's Directory Through Every Part of the Republic* (London: Edwards & Kibb, 1820), 493.

[11] Helen Kohn Hennig, ed., *Columbia, Capital City of South Carolina, 1786–1936* (Columbia: The State, 1966), 1–9, provides a synoptic review of the origins of the city, including quotations from the *Statutes at Large*, IV, 751–52.

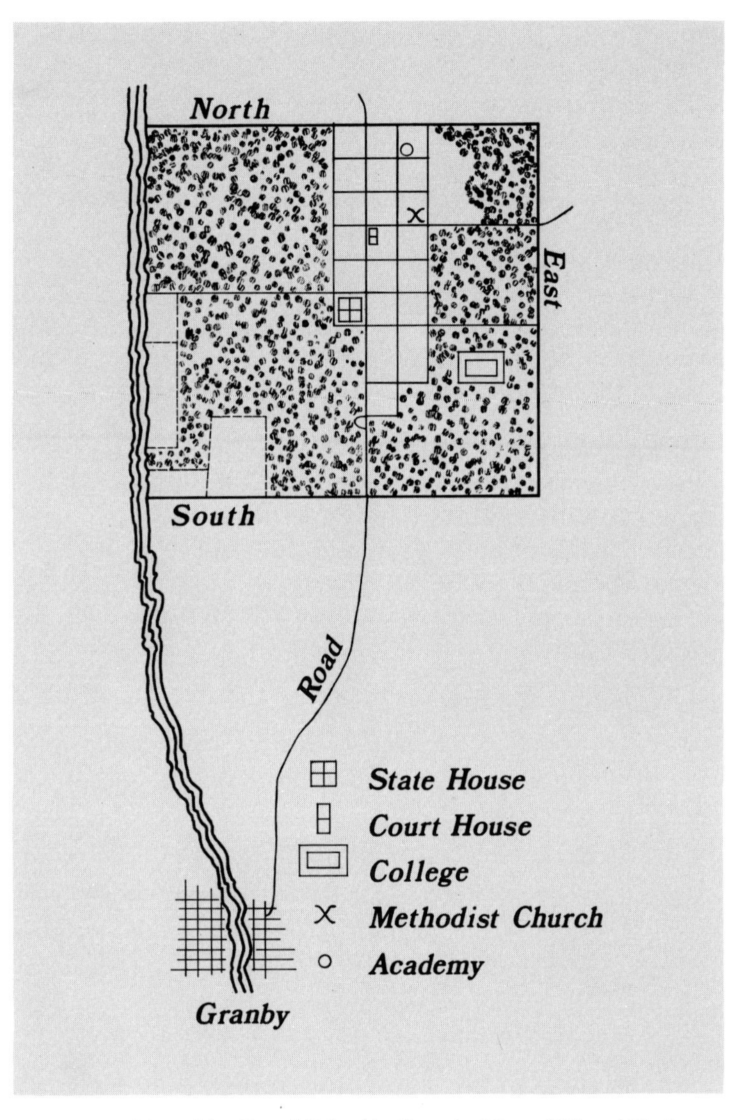

FIGURE 2. Map of the City of Columbia, from the *Diary* of Edward Hooker, 1805.

cipitous hills and dales, it lay below Richardson Street which marked the edge of the plateau; indeed, within twenty years of the original survey, Richardson Street was being referred to as "Main Street" by the city's inhabitants.

The commercial development of Senate Street, the proposed east-west boulevard leading from the river to the plateau, was irrevocably stunted from the outset. The foot of Gervais Street, only one block away, afforded a better site for a bridge. The chartering of the Columbia Bridge Company in 1819, expressly to erect the Gervais Street Bridge, effectively shifted subsequent attention away from the cnvisioned boulevard. Beyond this, the reserved public squares cannot have been, excepting the site of the Statehouse, in any way distinguished. Today we cannot demonstrate where these lands were located, or even ascertain that they were ever specifically set aside. It is clear, however, that the proposed squares were not conceived as foci or termini to balance the centrality of the Statehouse, to dramatize the configuration of the plateau, or to relate spaces and uses within the new capital city.

In short, the simplicity of Columbia's plan does not compare favorably with Williamsburg, Virginia, for example, which was laid out in 1699 by Francis Nicholson (1655–1728). Here one finds a composition that includes the orderliness of a grid system, the utility of radial streets and the visual impact of civic squares. The principal axis of the Williamsburg plan is the Duke of Gloucester Street which is terminated at its eastern end by a public square and the capitol, and at its western end by the college. Williamsburg, however, is exceptional, and one notes in defense of the men responsible for Columbia's checkerboard pattern that they were merely following the fashion of the day.

European tourists at the close of the eighteenth century often described with approval the prevalence of straight streets intersecting at right angles in America. Thus Francis Baily, writing in 1796 says: "This is a plan of which the Americans are very fond, and I think with reason, as it is by far the best way of laying out a city. All the modern-built towns in America are on this principle."[12] As Baily's tour progressed his opinion of the grid system changed, and upon arriving in Cincinnati he writes:

> I have taken occasion to express my approbation of the American mode of laying out their new towns, in a general way, in straight lines; but I think that oftentimes it is a sacrifice of beauty to prejudice, particularly when they persevere in making all their streets cross each other at right angles, without any regard to the situation of the ground, or the face of the surrounding country; whereas, these ought certainly to be taken into consideration, in order that a town may unite both utility and beauty; and with a little attention to this, a town might still preserve the straight line, and yet avoid that disgusting appearance which many of the new towns in America make. For it not unfrequently happens that a hill opposes itself in the middle of a street, or that a rivulet crosses it three or four times, thereby rendering its passage very inconvenient.[13]

This latter passage might have been written in reference to the Columbia plan, or even specifically about the gaping ravine which forms the eastern end of Senate Street.

The report which the Site Selection Committee made to the College Board of Trustees on Monday, 24 May 1802, offers the earliest evidence that the new city plan was inadequate. The college complex was the second major architectural undertaking in the new community, and we would expect the campus to occupy a prominent location. However, as has been suggested, no such setting was inherent in the plan. Consequently the committee recommended a location which was neither physically nor visually related to the Statehouse or to the major boulevards. The committee reported

> That in fixing upon a proper Site, whereon to erect the College at Columbia, they have met with considerable difficulty. The law establishing said College empowers to make choice of any Square or Squares of land yet unsold, for the purpose of erecting thereon the necessary Buildings, under this restriction, your Committee could not please themselves fully, and at the same time comply with the Law. . . . Amongst the unsold Squares in the Town of Columbia, there is not at present any Two or more Squares lying nearly contiguous, which would be Eligible Sites for said College. Your Committee anxious, however, to have so valuable an Institution located and speedily organized, would be unanimous in favor of erecting said College on a public Square, known by the name of Moultrie Square in the plan of the Town of Columbia, was it not that said Square lay too near a Mill pond now erecting by Mr. Purvis on Rocky Branch just above where the road leading from Columbia to Granby crosses the same—From this consideration your Committee beg leave rather to report a Square of land to the Eastward of the State House, as being the most eligible Site whereon to Erect the South Carolina College—Particular descriptions of the Sites referred to in this Report as also of the lands adjoining are herewith submitted.[14]

The "particular descriptions" appended to this report have not survived. However, the site described as being "most eligible" must have entailed problems, for the Board deferred action until their next meeting, scheduled for December 1802.

Plans for the buildings of the new college were being developed as the site was being chosen. We will recall that at the first meeting of the Board, Governor Drayton, as President of the Board of Trustees, was directed to "cause an advertizement to be made inviting artists to prepare and transmit to him under seal, . . . original Plans suitable for the erection of a College. . . ."

[12] John W. Reps, *The Making of Urban America, A History of City Planning in the United States* (Princeton: Princeton University Press, 1965), 294.
[13] Idem.
[14] Trustees' minutes. SCL.

Previous histories of the College treat this design competition only in passing. Here, we will explore it in some detail, for its results established a pattern which molded the subsequent architectural development of the College. It was natural that the Board should advertise for design proposals. In 1802 there was no state or national architectural organization for them to contact; indeed, architecture as a profession did not exist in America. Throughout the first three quarters of the eighteenth century, persons desirous of building something more elaborate than a vernacular structure had to rely upon either imported architectural pattern books or upon itinerant designers. The importance of the pattern books for craftsmen and dilettantes alike can be demonstrated by a correlation between extant colonial buildings and contemporaneous pattern book illustrations. The role of the emigrant designer throughout the colonies is evidenced in the work of such men as John James and John Smibert in Massachusetts, James McBean in New York, James Porteus in Pennsylvania, William Buckland in Maryland, John Ariss in Virginia, and John Hawks in North Carolina.

As the century progressed there was an evolution toward an organized architectural profession, and we find during the 1780s and 1790s that with increasing frequency individuals claiming to be specialists advertised the establishment of offices and offered to design buildings for a fee. Thus,

HOBAN, JAMES—Several applications being made to the subscriber, has induced him to establish an evening school, for the instruction of young men in Architecture, to commence the 3rd day May next. From the experience he has had, and the testimonial approbation of one of the first academies of arts and sciences in Europe, he hopes to merit the sanction of the public, and give satisfaction to his employers. Terms and hours of attendance will be made known at No. 43 Trott Street. He refers to the following gentlemen for his abilities: Thomas Gadsden, Geo. A. Hall, Roger Smith, David Cannon, Esquires. Plans, elevations, sections of buildings, etc, drawn at a short notice, and the different branches of carpentery executed on the lowest terms and most approved manner by Hoban & Purcell. —Charleston City Gazette and Advertiser, May 4, 1790.[15]

MYERS, CHRISTOPHER—Architect, Engineer, and Land-Surveyor, Regularly bred under his late father, Architect to the Board of Works in Ireland, and was clerk to Sir William Chambers, architect, for some years, respectfully takes this method to offer his services to the public —he has respectable testimonials of his abilities for the inspection of any gentlemen that may please to honor him with a call. Philadelphia, Nov. 20. Sassafras street, No. 177. —Federal Gazette (Philadelphia) Nov. 20, 1795.[16]

BANNER, PETER—Architect and builder from London designs and executes buildings of any description; by contract or otherwise, and also repairs and improvements of all kinds on reasonable terms. —New Haven, Sept. 3, 1798.[17]

BOWES, JOSEPH—Architect, Lately arrived from Europe, Begs leave to inform the Public in general, that he intends following the business of Architecture in all its departments; those therefore that are induced to take as well as utility, he hopes will be his promoters, and may be accommodated for anything in the Building Line, by applying to him at his lodgings, No. 13, Cherry alley, Philadelphia. N.B. As he has been a Draftsman for several years past, to the celebrated Robert Adams, Esq. Architect in London, He flatters himself that the Public will have no reason to doubt his abilities in that line, and in order to shew in some measure the opportunities he has had in the service of this Great Man, he will here take the liberty of inserting a few of the

[15] Alfred Coxe Prime, ed., *The Arts & Crafts in Philadelphia, Maryland and South Carolina, Gleanings from Newspapers, 1786–1800* (New York: Da Capo, 1969), II, 293.
[16] Ibid., 295.
[17] Elmer Davenport Keith and William Lamson Warren, "Peter Banner, His Building Speculations in New Haven," *Old Time New England*, the Journal of the Society for the Preservation of New England Antiquities, LIII (April–June, 1963), 102.

most remarkable Designs made by him in the last year of his life—viz. A very extensive Bridewell, now building in Edinburgh. A Public Square, with an elegant Modern Church in it, at do. Several new intended streets at do. A very extensive building, called the Advocate's Library, at do. An English Chapel, in the Gothick style, at do. A great part of the New University now building at do. An Infirmary for Glasgow. An elegant Trades Hall for do. An Assembly Hall for do. A large Church for do. Some very elegant streets for do. One Public Square in London, now building. Besides a number of very extensive Houses for Gentlemen's Seats in the country. Drawing in Architecture, Landscapes, etc. taught also by Joseph Bowes. Those ladies and gentlemen who wish to study these noble Arts under the above person, are requested to apply to him at his lodgings in Cherry alley, betwixt Third and Fourth streets. Tradesmen will be taught from 7 till 9 O'clock in the evening upon reasonable terms. To commence teaching on Monday, the 27th inst. —Penna. Packet, Oct. 15, 1794.[18]

It was to men of this type that the Board directed their announcement of a design competition. A copy of that advertisement appeared in the *Washington Federalist* on Saturday, 27 March 1802, which stated:

SOUTH CAROLINA COLLEGE.

In pursuance of a resolution of the board of trustees of the South Carolina College, Notice is hereby given that a premium of three hundred dollars is offered for the best original plan of a College, which shall be transmitted under seal to the president of the board, on or before the 4th Monday in May next, and which on examination may be approved of and accepted by the board. In projecting the said plan, due attention must be paid to the expence of erecting the same in stone or brick, at Columbia, in this state, which must not exceed fifty thousand dollars; and the building must be so calculated as to be capable of accomodating the greatest possible number of students, besides having rooms adapted to the studies and exercises of the institution, and for the accomodation of the Professors. The Premium will be paid to the author of the best original plan, which on being received is approved by the Board, as meeting the purposes hereby required.

By order of his Excellency John Drayton, Governor and Commander in Chief of this state and President of the Board.

(Signed) DANIEL HUGER,
Private Secretary to his
Excellency the Governor

—South Carolina, Charleston, 15th Feb. 1802.

The public notices elicited a number of responses. When the Board met to consider these proposals on Monday, 24 May 1802, it was resolved that "a select committee of three, be appointed to consider & arrange the plans proposed for a College; and to report thereon to the Board at their next Meeting. The Committee are Judges Grimkie, Johnson & Col. Hampton. The Board then adjourned until Tomorrow."

The next day when the Board reconvened at the governor's home, the select committee "informed the Board, that they were not yet ready to Report . . . the Board was consequently adjourned." We are able to glimpse something of the materials dealt with by the select committee through a partial list of the contestants which can be extracted from the Minutes of the Board. Six "artists" are mentioned by name—"Bolter, Clark, Mills, McGrath & Nicholson & Smith"—in the report of the committee. Elsewhere in the Minutes we find the names of "Asa Messer of Providence," "Mr. Smith the President of New Jersey College," "Mr. C. Perkins of North Carolina" as well as "Peter Banner of Boston" identified with correspondence concerning the competition. Beyond these contestants, the participation of Benjamin Henry Latrobe* and Benjamin Silliman can be established through surviving documents.

[18] Prime, *The Arts and Crafts*, 290.
*See Appendix.

Who were these men, and to what extent can we reconstruct their proposals? Nothing is known, either personally or professionally, about "Bolter," the only enigma on the list. Fortunately we possess signed and dated drawings submitted by Robert Mills (1781–1855), Hugh Smith (1782–1826), Peter Banner (1794–c. 1828) and Benjamin Silliman (1779–1864). Much is known about them and about aspects of their experience which influenced their proposals. Full statements by Benjamin Henry Latrobe (1764–1819) and Benjamin Silliman have survived concerning the contest. Finally, the observation of extant buildings substantiates hypotheses concerning the contributions of Edward McGrath (professionally active c. 1800–1803), Asa Messer (1769–1836), S. Stanhope Smith (1750–1819) and C. Perkins (dates unknown). In short, we have the means to develop a remarkably full picture of materials reviewed by the select committee.

Surviving drawings known to have been reviewed by the committee include a set of plans (Figures 3 and 4) signed "Robert Mills Architect and Practical Builder & Eng, Washington 1802." The larger of these presents the front facade elevation and a ground plan; the smaller shows the rear facade elevation, an elevation labeled "end view," a transverse sectional elevation through the central bay, a cornice profile and a second story floor plan. Both drawings are meticulously lined in india ink, the body of the building being treated with a light blue-grey wash, the timber framing is picked out with a yellow wash, the entries tinted with an ochre.

Another elevation (Figure 5), signed "Hugh Smith Architect," suggests an unusually plastic facade. Here the "Principle Front" is composed around a complex, central pavilion, which in turn is flanked by wings terminating in projecting bays. No known plans or sections illuminate this drawing, which, like the two drawings by Robert Mills, is tinted with a blue-grey wash. This color treatment indicates that the designers anticipated that the structure was to be either constructed of stone or finished with stucco to resemble stone.

From "B. Silliman" we have a plan, accompanied by preliminary specifications and cost estimates. Apparently no related elevations have survived, but the schematic plan depicts a well-developed baroque composition, a structure in the form of a modified U (Figure 6). Silliman contemplated using the head of this horseshoe arrangement for public uses and the extending arms for dormitory space.

The largest body of drawings surviving from the competition are those submitted by Peter Banner. His plans and elevations of seven separate buildings are extant. None of the Banner presentations are tinted; they are all executed in dense, black india ink (Figures 7 and 8).

We have, then, a total of ten designs for buildings which were reviewed by the select committee. Beyond these pictures we know from the Minutes of the Board of Trustees that the correspondence —now lost—of "Asa Messer of Providence," "Mr. Smith President of the College of New Jersey" and "Mr. Perkins of North Carolina" was taken into consideration by the committee. "Asa Messer of Providence" was the third president of Brown University. Dr. Messer was a member of the faculty at Brown, teaching mathematics and natural philosophy, when the president of Brown, Jonathan Maxcy, resigned in 1802 to accept the presidency of the new South Carolina College. Upon the resignation of Dr. Maxcy, Dr. Messer became the president pro tempore and, in 1804, he assumed the presidency, serving with distinction until his retirement in 1826. "Mr. Smith" was Dr. S. Stanhope Smith who served as president of the College of New Jersey in Princeton from 1795 until 1812. We may assume that their correspondence reflected their experience with collegiate architecture. This hypothesis is bolstered by the fact that, in thanking "Mr. Smith," the Minutes of the Board

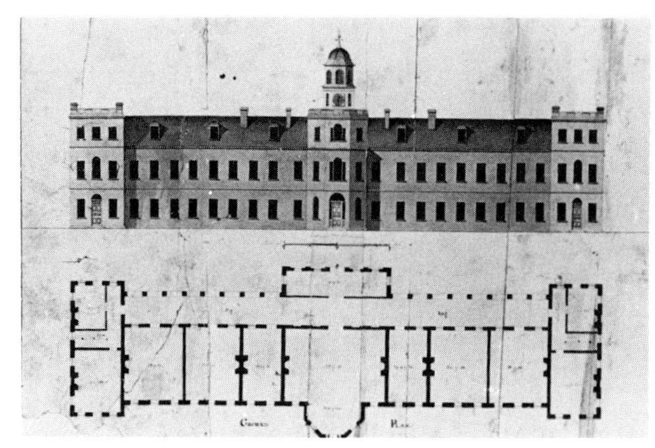

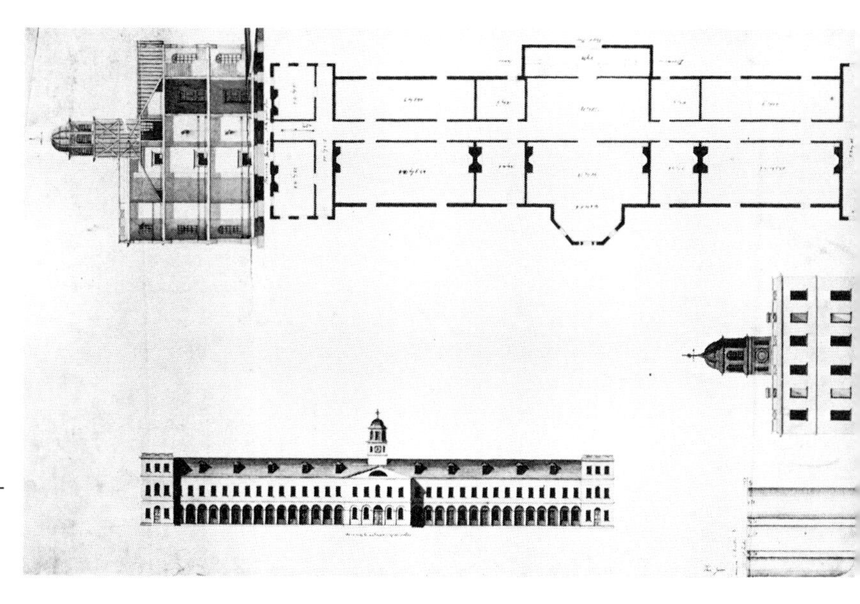

FIGURE 3 *above*. Proposal for the South Carolina College, signed "Robert Mills, Architect and Practical Builder, City of Washington, 1802," private collection.

FIGURE 4 *right*. Proposal for the South Carolina College, from the collection of the South Carolina Department of Archives and History.

make note of "certain manuscripts plans and considerations." Moreover, observation and comparison of the buildings at Princeton, Brown, and the South Carolina College confirm the formative influence of this lost correspondence. Our later analysis of the surviving drawings and a review of buildings related to the lost correspondence will put the cryptic references in the Minutes of the Board to "Mr. Perkins," to "Nicholson and McGrath" and to "Clark" into a meaningful perspective.[19]

In reviewing the initial building campaign, it should be noted at the outset that the select committee did not recommend the adoption of any of the proposals submitted. Instead, they drafted their own plan which was both presented and endorsed by the Board at the meeting of 26 May 1802. In accepting the committee report the Board

> resolved, that in the opinion of this Board neither of the artist's who have offered plans for the South Carolina College are entitled to the premium offered by the Board, because no plan proposed by them, has been adopted. But inasmuch as the plan adopted is founded upon some principles taken from the plans offered by Mr. Mills & Mr. Clark; and those artists have taken great pains to prepare an acceptable plan, the reward offered by the board in this advertisement, shall be equally divided between these two Gentlemen.

The committee report—the basis of this resolution—merits a close reading for it presents the criteria used to judge the submissions and suggests the design sources of the recommendation composed by the committee. The select committee which had been appointed to consider and arrange the plans proposed for a college reported:

> That after attentively considering the several plans rendered into the trustees they were of opinion that no one of them is sufficiently per-

[19] For biographical sketches of Asa Messer and Jonathan Maxcy see the *National Cyclopaedia of American Biography* (New York: James T. White, 1898), VIII, 21–22; the *Dictionary of American Biography* (New York: Charles Scribner's Sons, 1936), I, 344–45, reviews the life of Samuel Stanhope Smith.

FIGURE 5 *above*. Proposal for the South Carolina College, signed "Hugh Smith, Architect, 1802," private collection.

FIGURE 6 *right*. Proposal for the South Carolina College, signed "B. Silliman," from the collection of the South Carolina Department of Archives and History.

fect in the internal arrangements, to be entitled to an exclusive adoption.

They have therefore from a view of the whole; from considering the letter of Mr. Asa Messer, & their own knowledge of the subject; thought proper to recommend to the Board certain principles on which in their opinion an appropriate Plan should be predicated.

1st The building should be calculated to accommodate one hundred students and three Professors; allowing two students to each room generally & three of the youngest to a few; and one room to each professor; this will require about forty eight rooms.

2d That as the Health and comfort of the students is a primary consideration, each room should be 24 feet long and 16 broad and open to the North & South—these dimensions will admit of two windows in each front and a Partition at eight feet distance from the north side; which will have a sitting room of 18 feet square and a smaller room of 16 feet by 8 feet; which may if thought necessary be subdivided into two Studies of eight feet square.

3d That to preserve order & discipline every six rooms should form a separate Division of the Building: that is, the Building should be three stories high & a stair case run up between every other two rooms; the Doors all opening on the Front of the building into an Entry Six feet wide, leading to the staircase and common to every two rooms—separating the House after this manner by Partition Walls run up through the Roof, will also be a great protection from Fire.

4th It will be necessary to have a Chappel or Hall forty feet by fifty feet. Two lecturing Rooms a Library and a few spare rooms that may be converted to very excellant purposes.

If the above Ideas are approved of, it will then be necessary to have a building of the following plan and Dimensions.

A center building fifty feet square; which will give you in the 1st story a hall 50 by 40 & leave a vestibule of 10 feet for the staircase; in the second story a lecturing room, & Library, & an Entry. The 1st story of the Center Building we recommend to be 28 feet high; the second 15 feet high. The Roof flat, or nearly so with a Balustrade for an Observatory & covered with sheathing paper etc.

5th We recommend that from the center Building there should extend two wings, one Eastwardly the other Westwardly, each, one hundred & sixty feet in length; these according to the above plan will furnish forty Eight rooms.

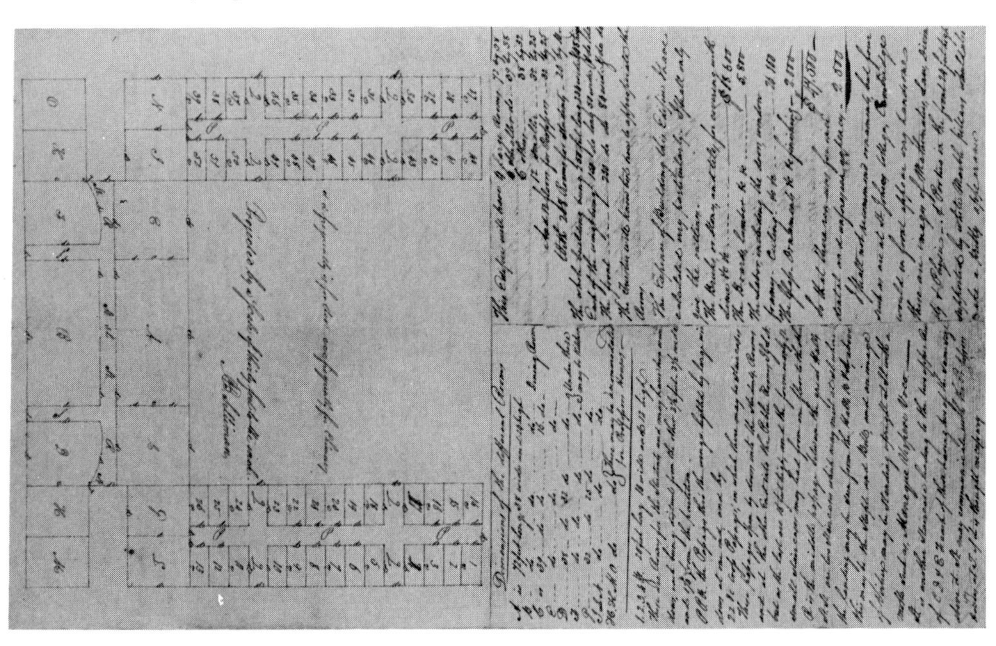

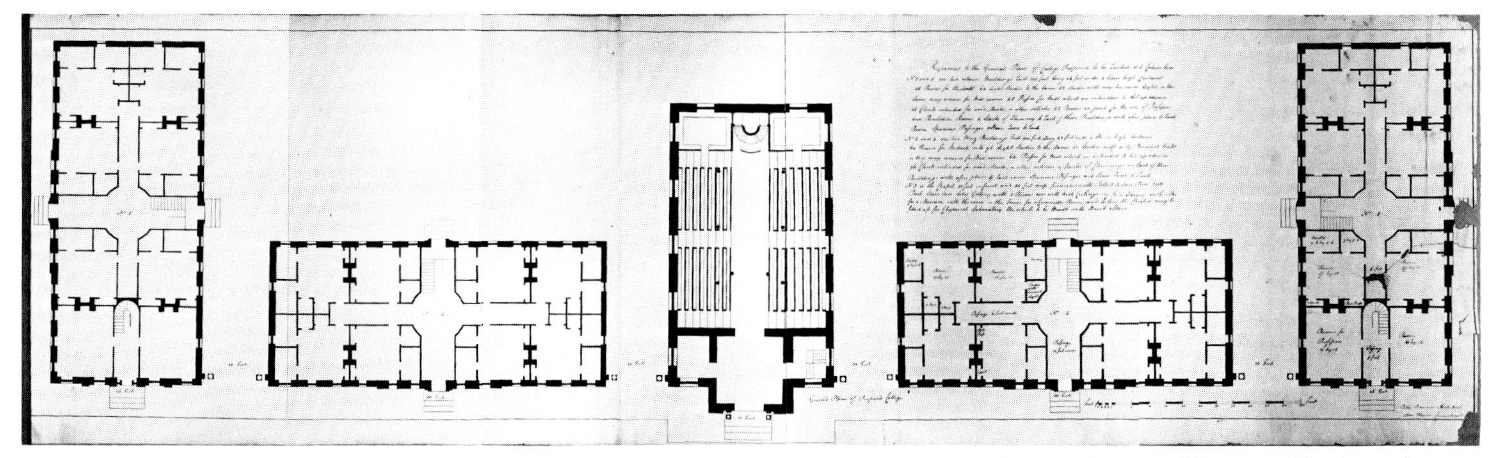

That the Foundation of the whole Building should be raised four feet from the ground leaving cellars in the foundation of six feet in height. That the first story of the wings be eleven feet high, the second be ten feet high and the third be nine feet high.

And that at some future Day when the Funds of the College will admit of it, a Balustrade shall be carried round the Roof, for which purpose it should be made as flat as possible, consistently with security from leaking and to be covered with slate or tile.

According to the above Plan, the width of the Wings must be twenty seven feet, and the Length & narrowness of the Building can be very handsomely relieved by means of Pediments judiciously placed.

6th With regard to the thickness of the Walls, your committee are of opinion that it will be sufficient to make the Foundation two & one half Bricks. The outer Wall of the 1st story . . . two Bricks. All the other Walls . . . one & one half Bricks.

7th Your Committee cannot dismiss this subject without warmly acknowledging their obligation to the artists who have favored them with Plans, particularly those gentlemen whose names are herein alphabetically written . . . viz. Bolter, Clark, Mills, McGrath & Nicholson & Smith—the designs which they have furnished afford

FIGURE 7 *above and right.* Two drawings of the proposal for the South Carolina College, signed "Peter Banner," 1802, from the collection of the South Carolina Department of Archives and History.

FIGURE 8 *below and left.* Three drawings of "Yale College" by Peter Banner, 1802, from the collection of the South Carolina Department of Archives and History.

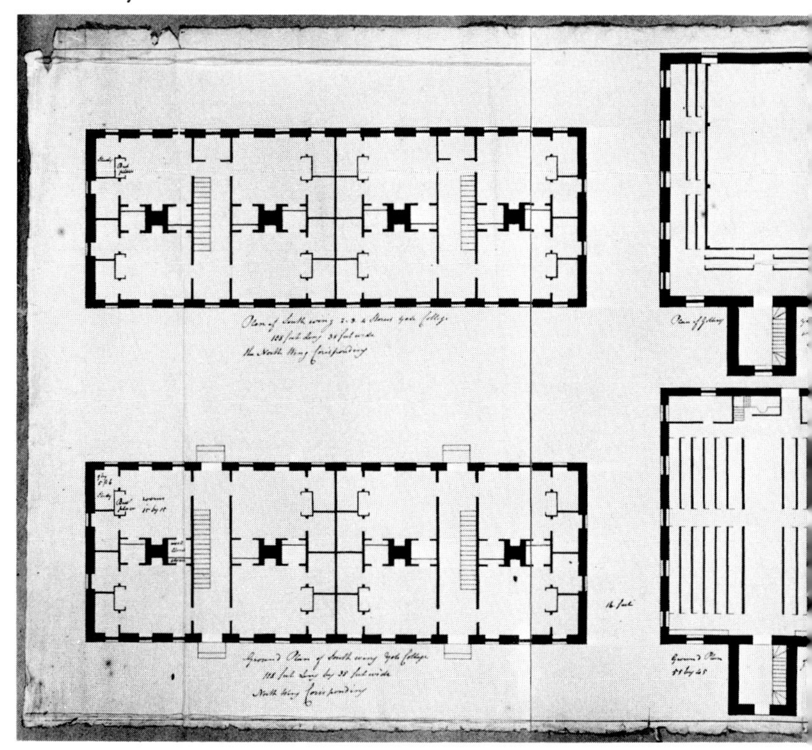

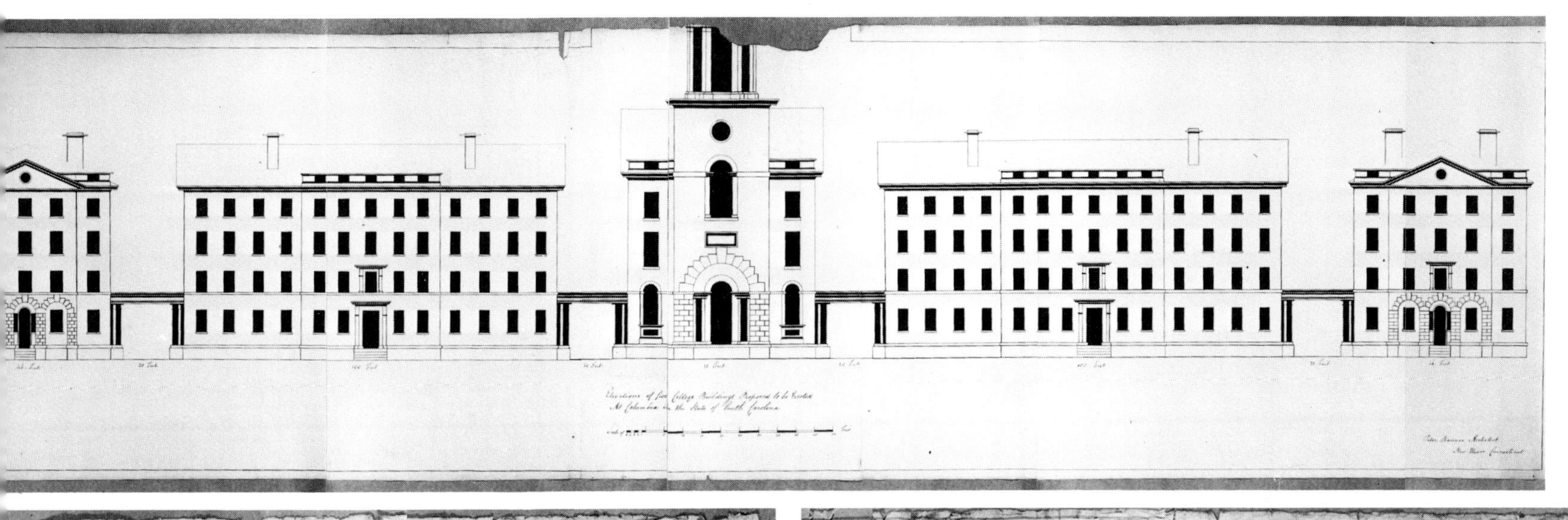
Elevations of five College Buildings Proposed to be Erected
At Columbia in the State of South Carolina

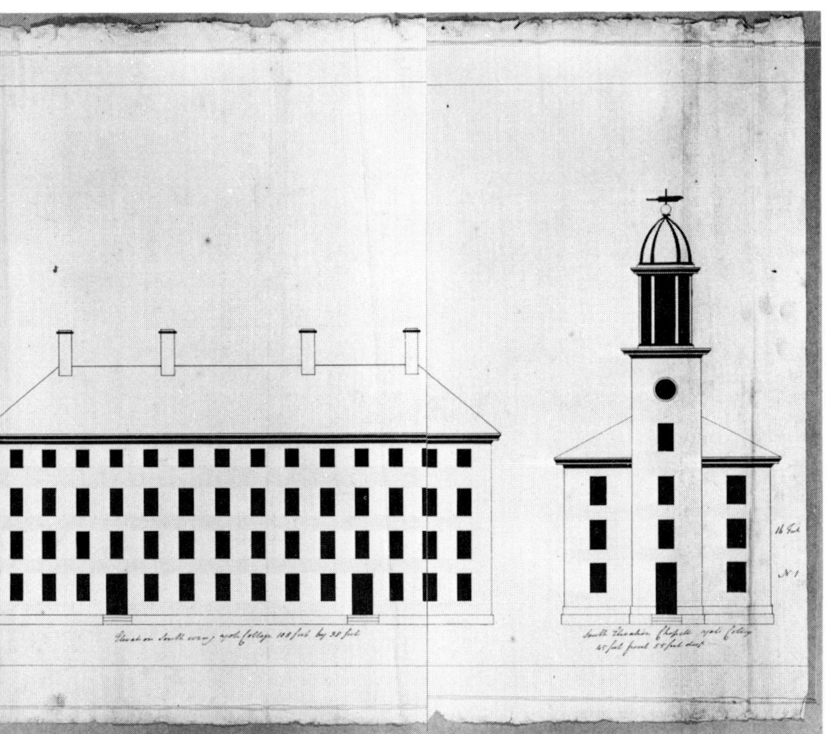

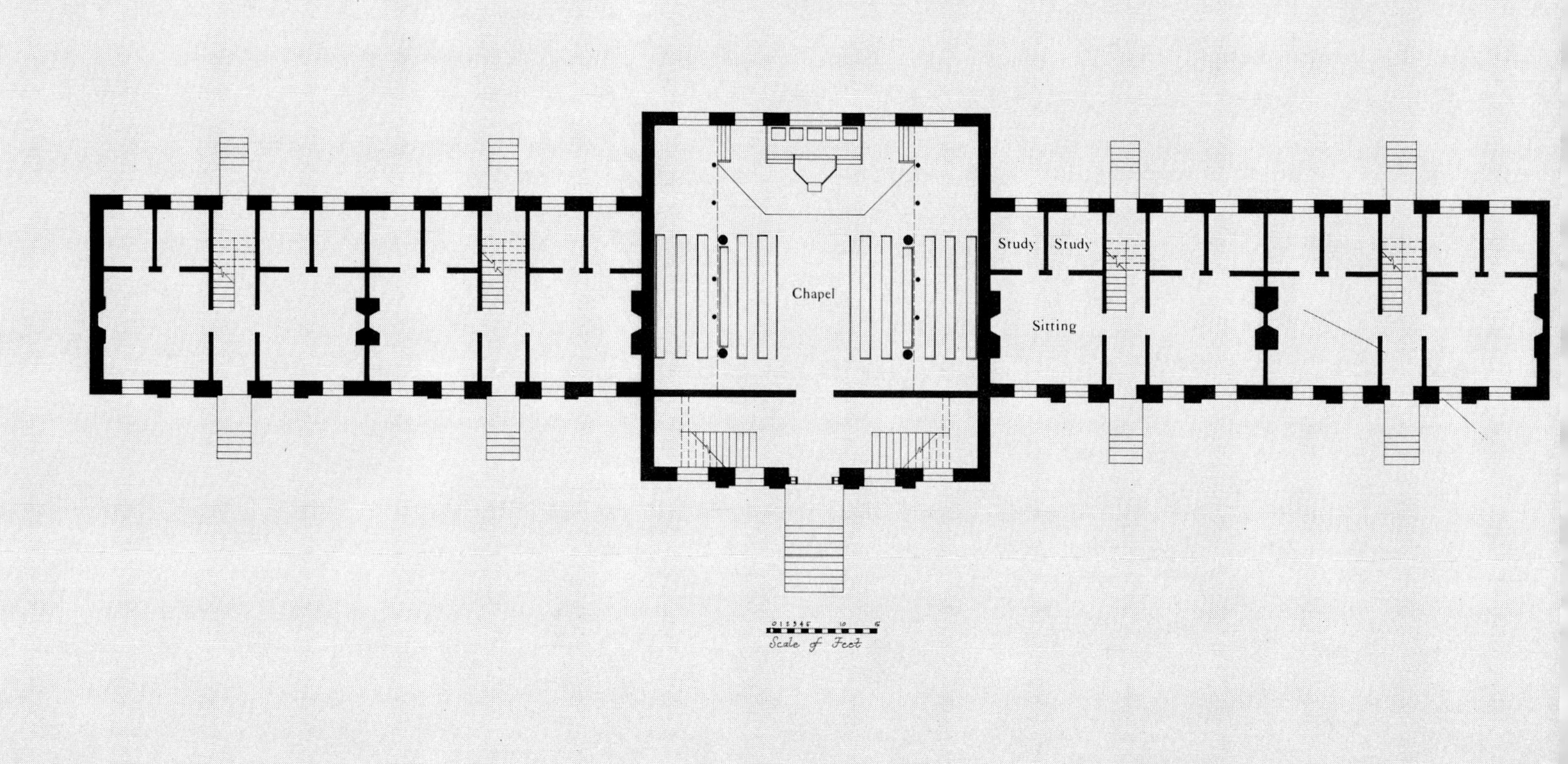

FIGURE 9. Ground plan of the building approved by the Trustees of the South Carolina College, a reconstruction by John Califf.

handsome specimens of American Talents, and if in Justice they feel themselves obliged to recommend Mr. Mills and Mr. Clark to the Board, on account of the Taste, Ingenuity & Variety of their designs, it is not without a sincere & hearty wish, that they had Premiums to bestow upon every one of the others above named—

As the Front Ornaments of the Buildings are not material to the internal arrangements, your Committee beg leave to submit the adoption of a Front to the Taste of the Board. [See Figure 9.]

One of the first things that this report brings to our attention is the fact that the committee's statement of principles effectively subordinates visual quality or style to functional qualities or "internal arrangement." The document begins with a statement of needs, then presents the disposition of interior space required to meet those needs, and finally, after touching on the use of balustrades and the placement of pediments, defers consideration of the "front ornaments" as immaterial to the task at hand. This utilitarian outlook is a recurrent theme in the architectural development of the South Carolina College. Given this bias, it is easy to understand the reluctance of the committee to approve the facade presented in the Hugh Smith proposal with its pilasters, columns, elaborate arcade and balcony, the ornate window treatment of its central block and, above all, the projection of the central block and the end bays.

To a lesser degree, similar criticisms might be made against the elevations by Robert Mills. In these we encounter a Federal Style building. The composition of its principal facade is based upon the balance of the central and terminal projections. The center of this axial balance is emphasized by the vertical alignment of the fanlight and sidelights of the entry, the Palladian windows, and the cupola. An effective reverberation of this alignment occurs in the more modest treatment of the entries and round-headed windows of the end bays. The primary features of the rear facade are the open pedestrian arcade and the central pavilion. The central pavilion with its windows recessed in arches, pilasters, belt course and fanlights in the pediment is an architectural pastiche of motifs drawn from the work of Charles Bulfinch. The open arcade, which would have been viewed as a waste of space by the select committee, is perhaps the most historically significant aspect of this design. Here Mills was providing covered communication and access to each of the classrooms on the ground floor. This design concept which was unprecedented in the new Republic antedates by a decade the colonnades which Thomas Jefferson designed to serve the same purpose at the University of Virginia.

The facades submitted by Peter Banner for the College are simpler than those proposed by Mills and Smith. In the Banner elevations there is little superfluity. Here the projecting elements, excepting the chapel bell tower, are merely one course of brick to create lines of shadow. The expanse of the exterior walls is not broken by ornament; only the rustication about the three major entries, a narrow belt course, a cornice and the intermittent appearance of a balustrade relieve the severe pattern of the fenestration. In reviewing this proposal we must compare it with a rendering of buildings at Yale College which was drawn by Banner as an attachment to his submission. The existence of this attachment is not surprising when we note that Peter Banner was designing and supervising the construction of buildings for Yale when he submitted his proposal for the South Carolina College.

Verbal explanations, now lost, must have accompanied these drawings, and we may presume that the thrust of Banner's commentary to the Board was to make explicit the relationships between his suggestions for the South Carolina College and the extant buildings at Yale. The central chapel in both instances is based upon the New England Old Style, with its characteristic projecting tower, rather than upon the more modish Wren-Gibbes formula of a portico surmounted by a spire. Beyond this, in the elevations of both the Yale chapel and the Carolina proposal, Banner portrays a similar disposition of solids and voids. Indeed, the only prominent difference between their chapels lies in the elaboration of the entry and the use of round-headed windows in the Carolina proposal. In plan, the Carolina chapel is much more complex, having a vestibule, an enclosed stairway, pews or benches mounted in tiers along the outer walls, and a semicircular balcony springing from a gallery on the entry wall. Beyond this, in the Yale dormitory plan, as we shall see, we find a rudimentary version of the dormitories adopted by the Board for the Carolina building.[20]

These elevations and plans by Peter Banner of the extant buildings at Yale College are the least ornamented, most utilitarian buildings surviving among the competition drawings. Knowing that the Board would have looked favorably upon something plain and simple, we might compare the renderings of Yale with the building recommended by the select committee and approved by the Board. Drawings for this building recommended by the select committee are unknown, except through a documentary reference found in the Executive Journal of Governor John Drayton:

> Charleston July 16th, 1802
>
> Sir:
>
> I have the pleasure herewith to transmit you, an elegant elevation of the So. Carolina College on the plan determined on by the board of Commissioners with a [*illegible*] letter accompanying the same, by Mr. Mills of Washington: also, plans for the Presidents & Stewards houses.
>
> You will be so obliging as to present it to that committee of the board of Trustees on that subject; of which you are chairman; and when they shall have considered it, I request it may be returned to me. The Board determined that all the plans were to be retained, & not given up to the different architects: consequently I request the return of Mr. Clark's plan which the committee are in possession of as soon as convenient.
>
> I am sir
> respectfully yours
> JOHN DRAYTON
>
> Hon. Tho. Gaillard
> Chairman of the Committee
> of the Board of Trustees
> of the So. Carolina College[21]

Our interpretation of this document suggests that upon reaching their decision, the Board directed Drayton to retain Robert Mills to draft the working drawings for the first of the college buildings. Be that as it may, the description of the structure found in the Minutes of the Board allows an accurate reconstruction of the basic ground plan approved on 26 May 1802. The dormitory wings of our reconstruction and the Yale dormitory building plan are markedly similar. This congruity cannot be coincidental: Banner's drawing must have provided the model for this aspect of the building proposed by the select committee. Architecturally, and thus socially, the major implication of the Yale building was the grouping of apartments or suites into a single tenement, for this had the effect of subdividing the occupants into intimate, socially cohesive groups. This pattern determined the nature of the living quarters in the first South Carolina College building, Rutledge College, built in 1805. Later, Rutledge was duplicated in DeSaussure (built in 1809), then again in Pinckney and Elliott Colleges (both built in 1837), and in Harper and Legare Colleges (both built in 1847). Clearly the ini-

[20] For the most extensive treatment of the work of Peter Banner see the series of articles by Keith and Warren in *Old Time New England*, XLV (April–June, 1955), 93–102; XLVII (October–December, 1956), 49–53; XLIX (April–June, 1959), 104–10; LVII (January–March, 1967), 57–76.

[21] *Executive Journal* of John Drayton. SCAH.

tial adoption of the Yale dormitory plan laid the foundations for much of the architectural development of the South Carolina College.

If this is the case, then why do the Minutes of the Board fail to mention Banner in recounting the competition? A possible explanation of this question is suggested in a communication from Governor Drayton to President Maxcy:

> Charleston, May 20, 1809
>
> An application made to me by Wm. Crafts as attorney for Mr. Banner of Boston to know why his account of $70.00 for drawing a set of plans for the college chapel and making a drawing of Yale College by the desire of the Board of Trustees of So. Carolina College, has not been paid; requesting that it should be done he says the account was laid before the board of trustees as appears by a letter from the late Gov. Hamilton at their meeting in April 1805.
>
> I request you will give me such information on the subject; as may enable me to answer the application made to me.[22]

This communication was not acted upon, and although Banner's "application" to Governor Drayton does indicate that the Board solicited his drawings of Yale, there is no evidence that he was ever compensated for this work. Perhaps the Board did not acknowledge the influence of Banner's submissions or pay him for his work because they viewed the Yale plans as being in the public domain. From available records we must assume that the Board was remiss in refusing payment, and it is understandable that Banner felt sufficiently aggrieved to retain an attorney. Nevertheless, there is a satisfying irony in this situation, for the designs that Banner submitted to the Board basically represented the efforts of other men.

Peter Banner was the builder, but not the designer, of the dormitories at Yale. The Yale dormitories were designed by John Trumbull (1756–1843), who is remembered primarily for his portraiture of the founding fathers. In 1792 Trumbull was painting in Philadelphia, then the capital of the United States, when the Treasurer of Yale, James Hillhouse (1782–1832) requested him to draft plans for new campus buildings. Hillhouse transmitted Trumbull's designs to the Rev. Ezra Stiles, the President of Yale, with a letter saying, "the proposed plan would be attended with an Air of Elegance and beauty beyond anything in America and I think combine economy and convenience. . . . I pay great deference to the opinion of Mr. Trumbull who appears to be perfect master of the Subject, and attentively to have improved the great opportunities he has had for making observations."[23] In April 1793, the cornerstone of Union Hall was laid; the structure was considered to be complete on 10 October 1794, when President Stiles accepted the keys. In short, it is John Trumbull's design for Yale's Union Hall that molded the nature of the student dormitories at the South Carolina College.

The buildings by Trumbull and the proposals by Banner do not suggest a central block and flanking wings. Consequently, in tracing the origins of the interior plan of the South Carolina College dormitories we do not explain the basic tripartite composition of Rutledge College. This tripartite formula had currency along the seaboard at the outset of the nineteenth century—one thinks of the design (Figure 10) by Charles Bulfinch for the Boston Almshouse (1799–1801). Closer to home, a similar building was designed in 1792 by Thomas Bennett (1754–1814) for the Charleston Orphan House (Figure 11). These designs by Bulfinch and Bennett are remarkably alike. Both of them were demolished during the nineteenth century, but we know that both charitable institutions housed tenants in their wings, reserving the central blocks for larger meeting rooms.

[22] Idem.

[23] Theodore Sizer, "John Trumbull, Amateur Architect," *Journal of the Society of Architectural Historians*, VIII (July–December, 1949), 3.

FIGURE 10 *above*. The Boston Almshouse, 1799–1801, by Charles Bulfinch, from an engraving by Abel Bowen reproduced from Caleb Snow, *A History of Boston*.

FIGURE 11 *right*. The Charleston Orphan House, 1792, by Thomas Bennett, from an engraving in the *Courier*, 13 October 1853.

In both form and usage these structures may be viewed as prototypes for Rutledge College, and given the prominence of Charles Bulfinch this is a seductive, intriguing hypothesis, but we need not embrace it as the truth. Instead we might seek the source of the dormitory wings and the public usage of the central block in the "manuscripts plans and considerations" received by the Trustees from "Mr. Smith, President of the College of New Jersey." This is more plausible, for the principal building at the College of New Jersey, Nassau Hall, built in 1756 (Figure 12), is a tripartite composition and bears a close resemblance to the original exterior of Rutledge.[24] Moreover, we know that Dr. Smith, prior to becoming the President of the College of New Jersey, had demonstrated his preference for this collegiate building type. In 1773 he resigned a teach-

HE SIXTY THIRD ANNIVERSARY OF THIS INSTITUTION WILL BE CELEBRATED ON TU
DAY, the 18th inst., at the Orphan's Church, Vanderhorst-street. The Rev. Clergy of all denominations,
or and Aldermen, the Officers and Commissioners of the several Boards under the authority of the City Co
and the citizens generally, are respectfully invited to join the Commissioners and the Children of the Institu
e New Alms House, Upper Wards, at 10 o'clock, and proceed in procession to the Orphans' Church, wh
ne Service will be performed, and an address delivered by the Rev. Mr. CUTHBERT.
The Procession will move at half-past 10 o'clock, from the Alms House. Masters who have taken App

ing position at the College of New Jersey and founded in 1776 the Hampden-Sydney College in Hampden-Sydney, Virginia. Here he built a replica of Nassau Hall as the first building of his new college.

A constellation or pattern begins to emerge from these bits of circumstantial evidence when we recall that Nassau Hall, which was the earliest building of this type in the colonies, was extensively imitated during the latter part of the eighteenth century. During the 1760s Nassau Hall influenced the designs of both Hollis Hall and Harvard Hall at Harvard (Figure 13). Then in 1770 we find that University Hall (Figure 14) at Brown was designed specifically "to be the same plan as that of Princeton."[25] In 1791 Dartmouth Hall

[24] For the complete history of Nassau Hall, see Henry Lyttleton Savage, ed., *Nassau Hall, 1756–1956* (Princeton: Princeton University Press, 1956), for a more superficial treatment, see John Fitzhugh Millar, *The Architects of the American Colonies, or Vitruvius Americanus* (Barre: Barre, 1963), 128–40.

[25] A letter from the Reverend James Manning to the Reverend Hezekiah Smith, 12 February 1770, quoted by Savage, *Nassau Hall*, 37, note 19.

FIGURE 12.
"A North-West Prospect of Nassau Hall," from an engraving by W. Tennant, from the collection of the Library of Congress.

(Figure 15), the first building on the Dartmouth campus, extended the influence of Nassau Hall into the forested mountains of New Hampshire. The relationship between Nassau Hall and Dartmouth brings to mind that reference in the Minutes of the Board of Trustees to "Mr. Perkins of North Carolina" and the plan he submitted "of Dartmouth College in that state." Perhaps Mr. Perkins' plan—for which the Board paid him eight dollars—depicted Old East (built 1793) at Chapel Hill, North Carolina, for its ground plan is similar to the dormitory wings of Dartmouth Hall.

Beyond whatever inferences one may draw from references to lost correspondence or from the physical resemblance of Nassau Hall and Rutledge College, we bolster the case for a stylistic connection by noting that several members of the South Carolina College Board of Trustees knew the Princeton building well. Judge William Johnson, Dr. Isaac Alexander, and John Taylor were graduates of Princeton. Another Trustee, Henry Dana Ward, was a Harvard graduate and would have been familiar with the adaptations of Nassau Hall on the Harvard Campus. Finally, Governor John Drayton himself attended grammar school in Princeton, New Jersey, and in August 1779 he entered Princeton's freshman class. He did not remain there long, however, for the death of his father on 3 September 1779 necessitated his return to Charleston. Years later, faced with the need to design a college building, Drayton and his fellow Trustees may simply have determined that their own collegiate experience had provided an appropriate precedent.

HARVARD UNIVERSITY, CAMBRIDGE, MASS.
J.& F. TALLIS. LONDON & NEW YORK.

FIGURE 13 *left*. "Harvard University" from an engraving published by J. & F. Tallis, from the collection of the Library of Congress.

FIGURE 14. A view of Brown University, by Benjamin Buck, from the collection of the Library of Congress.

The Initial Buildings

Rutledge and DeSaussure Colleges, the Steward's Hall and the Houses of the President and Faculty

1802-1813

A basic building ground plan was adopted on 26 May 1802, but construction did not begin at once. Indeed, seven months elapsed before a site for the college was chosen by the Board. It was not until 1 December 1802 that the Board meeting in Columbia

> proceeded to make choice of a site for the buildings to be placed on and having chosen the squares in the Plan of Columbia comprised between Medium Street and Blossom Street and Between Sumter Street and Marion Street, and also the Square comprised between Richardson Street and Sumter Street and between Green Street and Devine Street, it was Resolved that the Committee on Contracts be authorised to pursue all necessary measures to procure a Title to the said squares and the parts of the several streets comprised between them and that any other member of the Board who shall attend their meetings shall be permitted to vote relative to this subject.

This choice included parcels privately owned and therefore required an amendment of the original enabling legislation. The legislature responded quickly to this need, and on 18 December 1802 passed

> an Act authorizing the Commissioners for disposing of the public land in the town of Columbia to deliver up certain bonds therein mentioned, and to convey certain squares to the Trustees of the South-Carolina College.
>
> Whereas the board of trustees of the College of South-Carolina, in locating the spot which appeared to them the most proper for the site of the above mentioned college, have discovered that parts of the squares comprised therein have been sold to private persons, who are willing to relinquish their purchases;
>
> Be it therefore enacted by the honorable the Senate and House of Representatives, now met and sitting in general assembly, and by the authority of the same, That upon the several persons herein after mentioned, who have purchased lots or squares in the town of Columbia, or their legal representatives, producing to the commissioners for disposing of the public land in the town aforesaid certificates from the board of trustees of the college aforesaid, that they have executed to them full and sufficient conveyances, in fee simple, of the squares and lots herein after particularly described, the commissioners aforesaid are hereby authorized and directed to cancel the following bonds, to wit: the bond of George Wade, for the purchase of two acres, making part of the square bounded by Richardson, Divine, Sumter and Green

streets; also the bond of William Cunnington, for the purchase of the square bounded by Sumter, Green, Marion and Medium streets; also the bond of Thomas Rhett Smith, for the purchase of the square bounded by Sumter, Blossom, Marion and Divine streets; also the bond of Ezekiel Pickens, for the purchase of the square bounded by Marion, Divine, Bull and Green streets; and also the bond of Barlee Smyth, for the purchase of the square bounded by Marion, Green, Bull and Medium streets.

And be it further enacted by the authority aforesaid, that the commissioners aforesaid shall be, and they are hereby authorized and directed to convey to the trustees aforesaid, in fee simple, the square bounded by Sumter, Divine, Marion and Green streets, in the town aforesaid; also the square bounded by Marion, Blossom, Bull and Divine streets; and the half square, adjoining Wade's purchase, bounded by Richardson, Divine, Sumter and Green streets, as aforesaid.

And be it further enacted by the authority aforesaid, That the trustees aforesaid shall be, and they are hereby authorized and empowered to stop up and inclose all or any part of Green, Marion or Divine streets, which are included within, and bounded by Bull, Blossom, Sumter, and Medium streets.[1]

This act allowed the Trustees to acquire the south side of the Horseshoe, and enabled them to begin the construction of Rutledge in the spring of 1802. Even before acquiring this land, the Board in anticipation of construction, had given thought to the exterior appearance of the building and had made preparations for executing building contracts. Thus, on 27 May 1802, the conceptual foundations for the ground plan of the Horseshoe as a whole were laid by the determination that

instead of the Building of one continued Front reported by the Committee, their shall be two Buildings fronting each other, at such a Distance apart, as will be suitable to the Land to be procured (say) not exceeding Three hundred feet; That they shall vary in nothing further —the plan reported except that the Center Buildings shall be no higher than the Wings. The Wings no more than Eighty feet in length. The

FIGURE 15. Dartmouth Hall, Dartmouth College, from a photograph by the author.

Center of one to contain a Chapel 24 feet high & a Suite of Rooms above it. The Center of the other to be of three stories and divided into as many Rooms as may here after be directed according to the Plan substituted.

Resolved that a Committee of Five shall be appointed in Charleston who shall decide upon the Stile in which the College shall be finished, and shall advertize for proposals to furnish materials and to erect the Building either in the whole or in part to be delivered in, on or before the first Monday in November next. The Committee consists of The Speaker of the House of Representatives, Judges Grimkie, Bay, Johnson & Trezevant. Resolved that the above Committee do deliver unopened all proposals received by them to the Board at its regular meeting at Columbia next.

Resolved that the President of the Board be requested in the Name of the Board to write to the different Person's who have furnished them with Plans & Communications, thanking them and expressing their Sense of Obligation for the same.

[1] *Acts of the General Assembly of the State of South Carolina from December, 1775, to December, 1804, Both Inclusive* (Columbia: D. & J. J. Faust, 1808), II, 475–77.

Here we have the earliest expression of the Board's intention to erect similar buildings "fronting each other" across an open space. This program of an architectural mirror image was to dominate the appearance of the Horseshoe until the middle of the nineteenth century. The early intention to erect more than one building is further evinced by the use of the plural in subsequent references to the pending construction. Thus, on 1 December 1802, the Board resolved that "the Committee on Contracts be permitted to deviate so far only from the General Plan as to elevate the walls of the Center Buildings above the walls of the Wings to a height not exceeding seven (?) feet."

The earliest known graphic reference to the disposition of these buildings upon the site is the sketch (Figure 16) which appears in the *Diary* of Edward Hooker. Writing on 6 November 1805 as the buildings were under construction, he has left us a simple plan and a description of Rutledge and DeSaussure Colleges and a projection of subsequent structures "to be built fronting each other, and ranging in a line with the first mentioned long buildings."

> This forenoon, I called on Mr. Hanford, and with him took a view of the college buildings which are erecting, on a pleasant rise of ground about ¼ of a mile southeast of the State House. The place though so near the center of the town is however very recluse; there being no houses around, and even the lands being uncleared and covered with lofty pines, and wild shrubs. The plan is to have two buildings of perhaps 160 feet in length each, facing each other at the distance of 160 feet apart. At right angles to these, and facing the area inclosed between them, it is proposed to place the President's house; and afterwards, as occasion may require, other buildings, such as the dining hall and professors houses are expected to be built fronting each other, and ranging in a line with the first mentioned long buildings. The buildings A and B are erected, and A is finished except the central part, which is however advanced so far as to be capable of use. The central parts are designed for the Chapel, Library, Philosophical Chamber, Recitation Rooms, etc.—the wings are designed for scholars' mansion rooms—C is the site of the President's house, D the place for a dining hall, E for a Professor's house perhaps.[2]

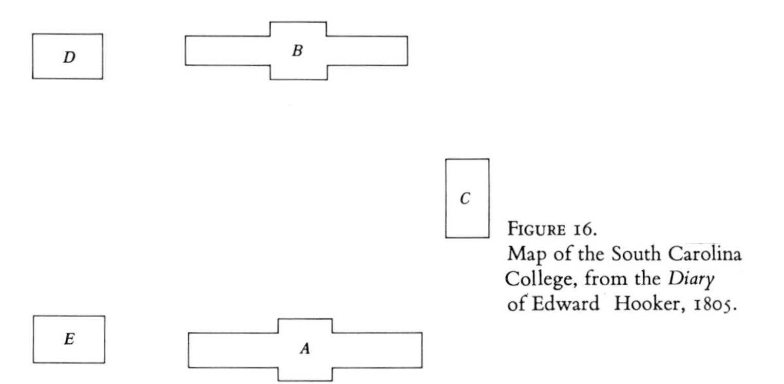

FIGURE 16.
Map of the South Carolina College, from the *Diary* of Edward Hooker, 1805.

These lines demonstrate that virtually from the outset the "horseshoe" concept governed the development of the South Carolina College.

Viewing the buildings through Hooker's eyes in 1805, we have broken the sequence of the architectural development of the College, and having done so, we should note that the Board had made provisions for obtaining building contracts at the same meeting at which they had selected a site for the College. Thus, on 1 December 1802, they had "Resolved that Col. Thomas Taylor Col. Wade Hampton, the Hon. Speaker of the House of Representatives the Rev. D. E. Dunlap and John Taylor Esq. be a Committee to contract for the Building of the College agreeable to the plan adopted either in whole or in part, also for furnishing materials requisite to compleat the said buildings either in whole or in part and that they do forthwith proceed to carry the resolution into effect."

[2] Hooker, *Diary*, 851–52.

Following this meeting a contract was executed by the committee for the construction of Rutledge and DeSaussure Colleges. Apparently, this seminal document has not survived. However, we may assume that it was effective prior to 26 April 1803, for on that date a "supplementary contract" was approved by the whole Board. Previous historians of the College have stated that the man who contracted for the construction of the initial buildings was named "Edward Clark."[3] This is wrong. It is true that there was a nineteenth-century architect named Edward Clark (5 August 1822–6 January 1902), but he was not associated with the establishment of the South Carolina College. Many references in the early records of the College note a "Mr. Clark" or "Mr. Clarke" and are clearly related to both the design contest and to the initial building contract, but those references which include a surname all mention "Richard Clark" or "Richard Clarke." For example, Richard Clarke is noted as "the undertaker" of the college buildings in the Board Minutes of 17 December 1806 and as "the College Architect" in the Minutes of 19 December 1806; Richard Clark is called "the undertaker of the College Buildings" on 20 December 1806 and appears again as the "College Architect" on 23 April 1807. In the frequent references to the initial contract, the name "Edward Clark" does not appear. Moreover, it is significant that no "Edward Clark" is listed in either the census records or the wills of Richland County during this period. On the other hand, the letters of administration for the will of Richard Clark were applied for on 30 June 1808, only two days after the last appearance of the name "Clarke" in the Minutes of the Board as an active participant in the development of the College.[4] We may conclude that it was this Richard Clark who was responsible for the first College building contract.

Little can be determined about Richard Clark (— –c. 28 June 1808) "Architect of the College Buildings." Was he, for example, the "Mr. Clark" who shared the design prize with Robert Mills? This does seem plausible, for if there had been more than one Mr. Clark involved in the early deliberations of the Board, it is probable that the Secretary would have distinguished between, or among, them through the use of surnames—as was consistently done in the case of the two Taylor brothers, John and Thomas. And Richard Clark was indubitably capable of design, for we know that his design proposal was accepted for the third building erected for the College—the Steward's Hall (1805–1806) which was constructed on the site now occupied by Harper College. Regardless of his participation in the original contest, we do have primary evidence which demonstrates that he had ties with Ireland, that he was active in Columbia from 1803 through his death in 1808, that his work for the College included both design and construction, and finally, that his relationship with the Board of Trustees was fraught with difficulties.

Richard Clark apparently began construction of Rutledge College during the spring of 1803, for in late April of that year, the Board established the procedural means for the disbursement of the building funds: "Resolved that the President [Judge Johnson] shall be and is hereby authorised and empowered and directed to procure from the Comptroller upon his own order any sum or sums not exceeding in the whole Twenty thousand Dollars out of the Treasury of this State to be applied for the purpose of discharging all

[3] Green, *History of the University*, 21; Hollis, *South Carolina College*, 27, 49; also see Beatrice St. Julien Ravenel, *Architects of Charleston* (Charleston: Carolina Art Association, 1964), 119.

[4] *Richland County Wills*, Vol. I, Book E, p. 51. SCAH. The will was witnessed by John Hooker, brother of Edward Hooker, and by Henry Preston Hampton and Isaac A. Johnson. The most interesting provision of the will is that among his effects he numbered "the rents and profits of a farm by the name of Ballartarsna in the parish of Tintern, Barony of Shelburne in the county of Wexford, and the Kingdom of Ireland."

FIGURE 17. The South Carolina College, c. 1827, a watercolor signed "T. Ulor," from the collection of the South Caroliniana Library.

contracts for completing the College as they become due."

Neither plans nor elevations related to the original construction of Rutledge College have survived. Nor do we have any reliable, contemporary descriptions of its exterior architectural features. Despite these lacunae, there are several means by which we can visualize its original appearance with some confidence. The watercolor by "T. Ulor" in the collection of the Caroliniana Society provides an oblique view (Figure 17) from the north of the facade as it existed c. 1820–1827. This view is most helpful in establishing the disposition of the blind triple arches which originally dominated the central block. The painting also presents the nature of the cupola and indicates that Rutledge was constructed with an exposed brick exterior, with white trim about the windows and doorways, and a slate roof. This view also plainly portrays the frontal gables or pediments which punctuated the dormitory wings. The value of the information contained in this painting is enhanced by the fact that Rutledge has been extensively modified since the painting was completed (Figure 18). The exterior of the building was stuccoed, scored, and painted to resemble stone, and the original triple arches, cupola and the pediments of the wings were all lost during the reconstruction which followed the fire of 15 February 1855. Due to these alterations, the original state of Rutledge can be visualized most readily through an examination of the buildings which followed its pattern.

FIGURE 18 *left.* Rutledge College, from a photograph by Judith Steinhauser.
FIGURE 19 *above.* DeSaussure College, from a photograph by Judith Steinhauser.

FIGURE 20. McCutchen House, from a photograph by Judith Steinhauser.

Thus, DeSaussure (Figure 19), the second building constructed, was erected as a mirror image of Rutledge. Its dormitory wings reflect the scale, the secondary blind arches and the frontal gables which existed, but which have been lost, on Rutledge itself. Unfortunately, the west wing of DeSaussure was destroyed by fire on 7 May 1851. Following this fire DeSaussure College underwent several renovations during the 1850s. In these restorations it too lost many of the exterior features seen in the Ulor painting.

Perhaps the most evocative evidence of the original impact of the central blocks of both Rutledge and DeSaussure is now the face of McCutchen House (1813) which was erected as a double house for the faculty. McCutchen (Figure 20) has also been stuccoed, but here we can still see the effect of the blind arches framing the windows and the entry of the principal story. Viewing McCutchen, we are able to envision the rhythm that this architectural device established when it served to unify the larger buildings—framing the entries and reverberating in the wings (Figures 21 and 22).

The responsibility for the design of the exterior of both Rutledge and DeSaussure was given to the "Committee of Five" (———[5], Grimke, Bay, Johnson, Trezevant). This committee worked without restraints other than those imposed by the ground plan and by the previous decisions of the Board to employ a low pitch on the roof (to facilitate the anticipated addition of balustrades) and to elevate the walls of the central blocks above those of the wings. Beyond the work of the committee it is possible that Robert Mills played a creative role as is indicated by the letter of Governor Drayton cited above.

[5] The "Committee of Five" established by the Board was really a committee of four. The fifth seat, which was to be filled by the Speaker of the House of Representatives, remained empty, pending an election, while the major decisions concerning the buildings were made.

FRONT ELEVATION

1/8" —— 1'-0"

FIGURE 21 *above*. Rutledge College, a reconstruction: research by John Califf, drawing by Wayne Young.

FIGURE 22 *below*. McCutchen House, a reconstruction: research by John Califf, drawing by Wayne Young.

0 1 2 3 4 5 10 15

Scale of Feet

FIGURE 23. Blacklock House, Charleston, South Carolina, from a photograph by Robert M. Smith, Photo-Vision, Columbia.

Although we lack a specific pedigree, a documented source of the facade of Rutledge and DeSaussure, we can understand these designs as products of their time. Several comparisons are useful in this regard. This wide elliptical arch flanked by smaller half-round arches had been used by Charles Bulfinch in Boston's triumphal arch for Washington, erected in 1789. For this occasion, Bulfinch appears to have adapted plate 8 of John Borlack's Design of Architecture for Arches and Gates. Subsequently, we find that the treatment of the entry of the Boston Almshouse by Charles Bulfinch (1799–1801) is quite similar to the arched motif used in the South Carolina College buildings. The scale and proportions of the same device on the Connecticut Statehouse (1793–1796) designed by Charles Bulfinch, is reminiscent of the dormitory wings of Rutledge and DeSaussure, and in the Blacklock House (1800) in Charleston, South Carolina (Figure 23), we find the same motif employed in a manner markedly similar to its appearance in McCutchen. A repeated appearance of one motif such as we find here suggests the current of cultural transfer. In this case, congruities are not surprising, for the ties between Boston and Charleston during the late eighteenth century were tantamount to the relationship between Charleston and Columbia. The blind arch, as used in these few buildings was an idiom of the English Adam Style which was a dominant force in American architectural design in 1800.

Other aspects of the South Carolina College buildings bear witness to the formative influence of this style. For example, all of the buildings erected prior to 1835 had flat, decorative panels of stucco, painted white to resemble limestone or marble, placed in their pediments and in some cases in the belt course between the principal and the second stories as well. This use of discretely framed decorative elements was a hallmark of the Adam or Federal Style, as was the severe, linear quality of the simple cornices and the general absence of projecting ornament. It is probable, of course, that in the final analysis the College owed its chaste design to its location in Columbia, inland where architecture was but a pale reflection of the taste and fashion of the coastal metropolitan centers.

Although the Board does not appear to have established a construction schedule, they must have been gratified by the progress made on Rutledge College, for by January 1804, only nine months after the work had begun, they were able to circulate a form letter to notify American academicians of the impending election of faculty. A public announcement was also circulated to newspapers at this time, and thus the *Repertory*, published in Boston on 10 February 1804, carried the following item on its front page:

> SOUTH CAROLINA COLLEGE
>
> With much pleasure we announce to our fellow citizens, that the buildings of this institution are in such forwardness, as to induce the Trustees at their last meeting to resolve, that they will proceed to the election of a President and a Professor on the 22d of April next. We believe that no seminary of learning in the United States, possesses more liberal endowments than this. The salary of the President is settled at 2,500 dollars, besides a house for his residence; that of the Professors of natural philosophy, etc. 1,500 each, and their board and lodging; and of each of the other Professors, 1000 dollars, and their board and lodging.
>
> The buildings will consist of two ranges, each 250 feet in length. The philosophical apparatus will be equal, if not superiour, to any collection in America; and the library will open with near 5000 volumes of the most select books, in all branches of learning. —The whole of which, we are informed, is expected out from London in the spring of the present year. The situation of Columbia for such an establishment is certainly very eligible; the buildings are erected on an eminence that commands a most extensive prospect, and form its elevation, insure free and salubrious circulation of air.

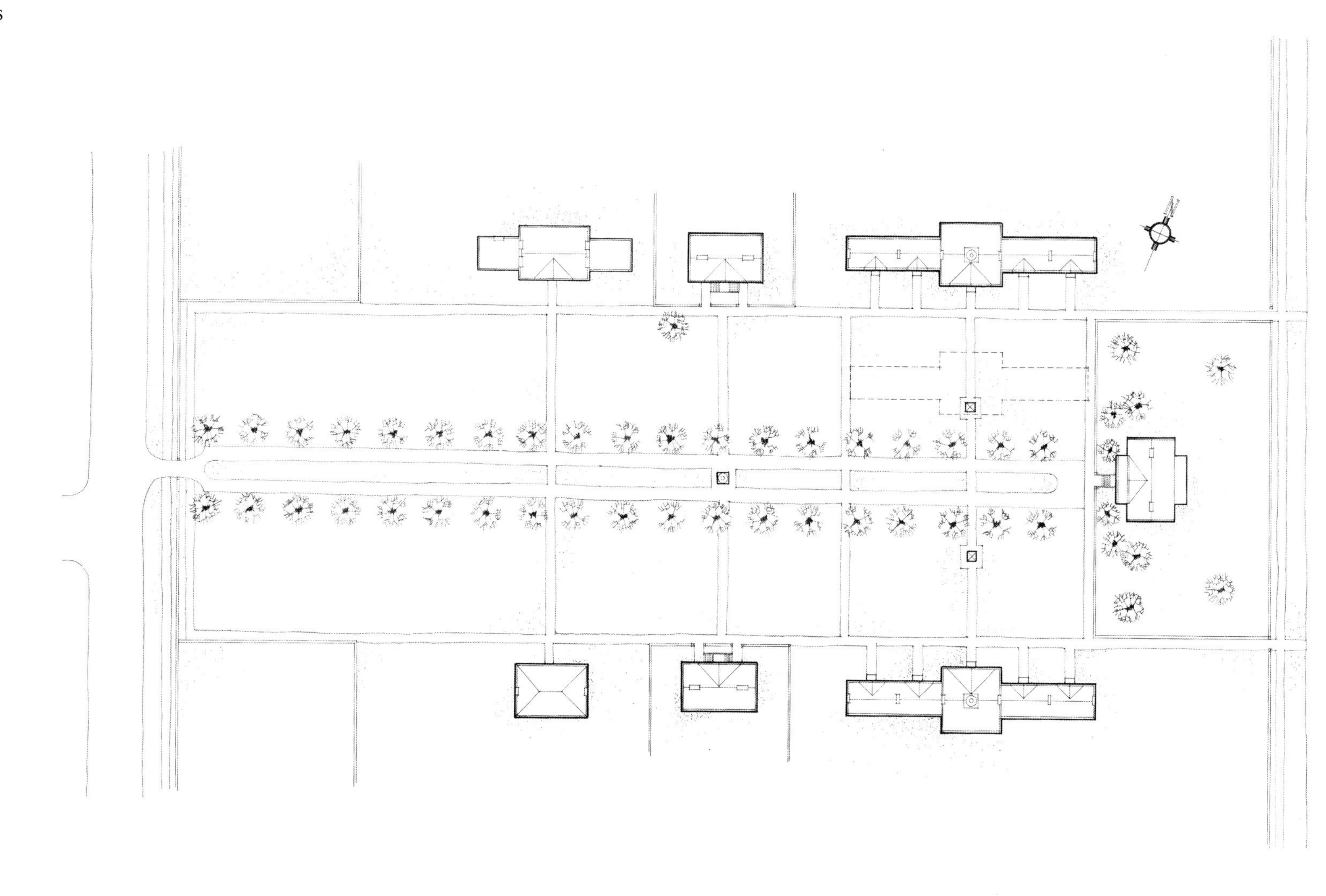

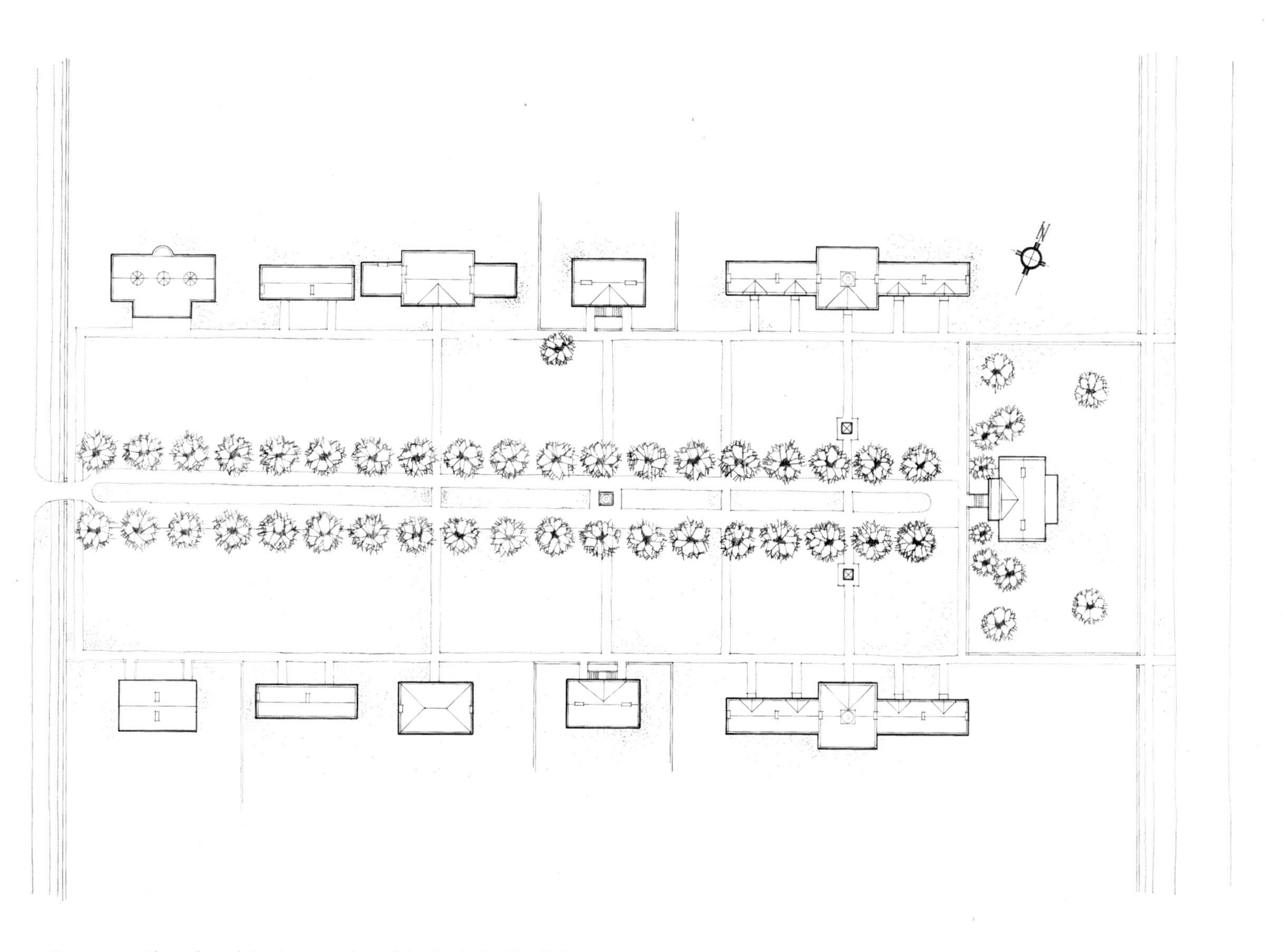

FIGURE 24. Chronological development plans of the South Carolina College (pages 38–41): research by John Califf, drawings by Alex James.

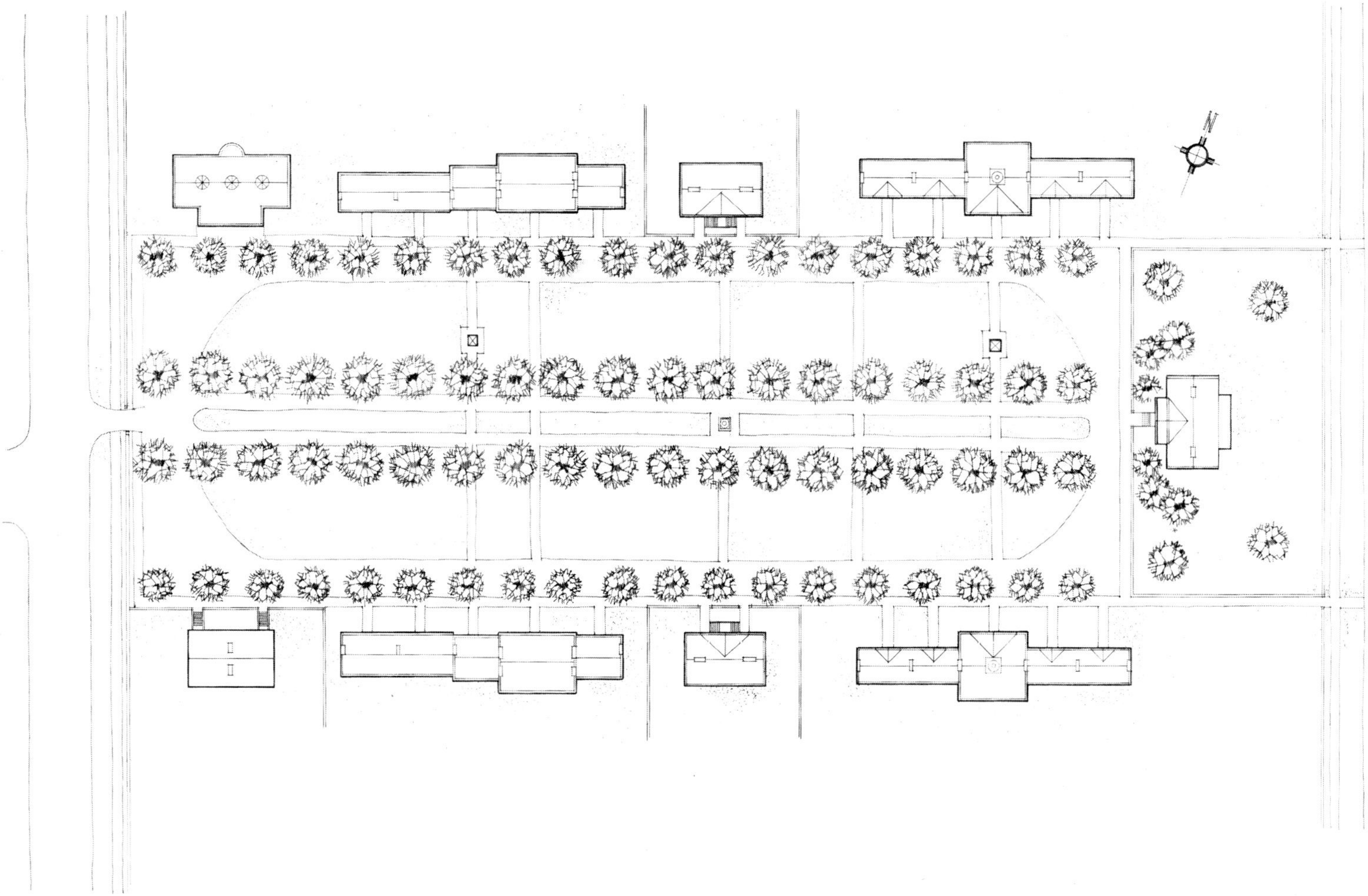

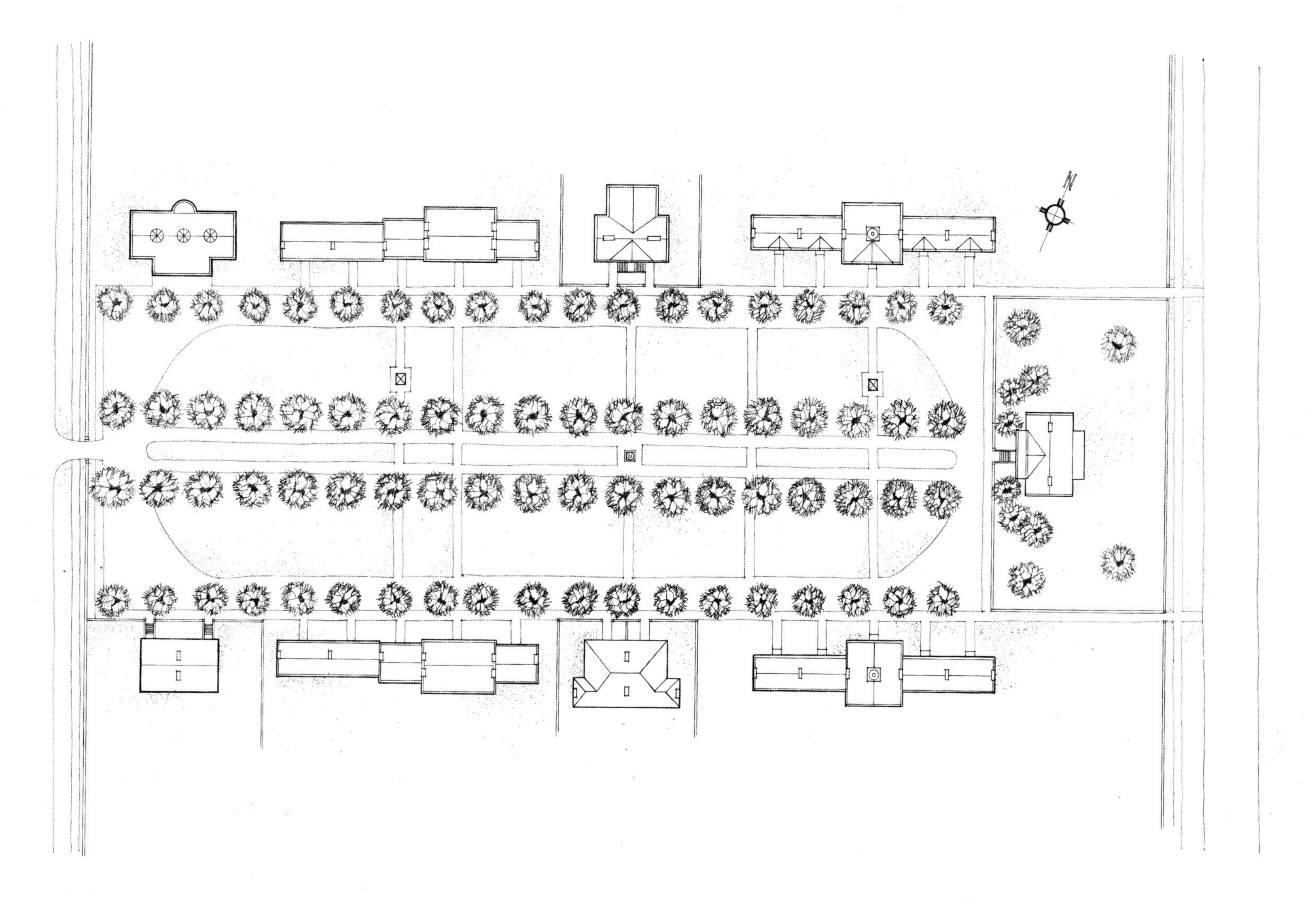

41
THE INITIAL
BUILDINGS

On schedule, at its April meeting of 1804, the Board elected a faculty and also resolved "that the standing committee be & are hereby directed to rent a suitable Dwelling house for the accommodation of the President of S. Carolina College, to be paid out of the monies in the hands of the college Treasurer." This measure was certainly necessary, for the provision of a President's residence, although promised in their advertisements, had not yet been formally discussed. Another architectural matter of concern at this meeting was the nature and placement of the second building, for although it had been previously determined to duplicate Rutledge, the Trustees now considered another configuration, and from the drift of this discussion we must conclude that the second building was not yet seriously under way.

> April 29, 1804 Resolved That the Building Committee be authorised if they deem it proper and Expedient to contract with the Architect of the College for the following alteration in the College Edifice. That instead of Two ranges contemplated, there shall be added two tenements (of the like extent with the Tenements in the wings) to each of the wings of the Building now erected. The end Tenements to be placed fronting East and West. Resolved also that in case the Building Committee shall not find it advisable to make the said alterations that the Foundation of the second Range shall be placed not less than three hundred feet from the Range of Buildings already erected.

This moment of indecision and reconsideration was a critical juncture in the history of the development of the College. Had the Building Committee elected to extend Rutledge—the first option offered them by the Board—then the first structure would have assumed a U form, much like the ground plan submitted by Benjamin Silliman in the design contest, and the subsequent growth of the campus would have been much different. However, they did not. They followed the second option, placing DeSaussure 320 feet away from Rutledge, and this placement established a building line that was adhered to by the remaining buildings. This building line had another effect. It established an east-west axis on the college ground which did not coincide with the east-west axis of the city streets. Creating this axis internal to the college grounds the committee effectively insured that Medium Street (now called College Street) would not traverse the campus, that the authority to close streets which had been granted by the legislature would be exercised. With the placement of DeSaussure decided, its construction was soon begun, and by the end of the year, on 6 December 1804, the Board was able to establish a committee to make "the necessary arrangements for putting the College in full operation on the tenth Day of January next" (Figure 24).

With a faculty of two and a student body of nine the College opened on schedule. DeSaussure then was only a shell with its exterior walls and roof completed, but with its interior partitions, stairs, flooring, and detailing untouched. Rutledge, on the other hand, was complete. Edward Hooker describes its finished interior saying,

> The central parts are designed for the Chapel, Library, Philosophical Chamber, Recitation Rooms, etc. —the wings are designed for scholars' mansion rooms. . . . That part of the work which is done is in a handsome, though not all in a durable stile. The chapel occupies the two lower stories of the central building on the right, and is in a beautiful style of workmanship both within and without. The Library room above is supported by four stately Tuscan columns, which rise from the area of the chapel with considerable majesty, and give to the room an appearance of grandeur. The galleries are supported by a row of smaller pillars. The room is nearly or quite square. The pulpit is surrounded by a semi-octagonal stage, on the right and left sides of which are steps leading to the officers' seats and thence are other steps to the pulpit. The upper tiers of windows are semi-circular at top, as

> in Episcopal churches and have some neat ornamental work about them. The stage, pulpit, staircases, bannisters, seats, etc. are all painted white, and make, now, a very chaste and pretty appearance; but I question if they will long remain so. There are but a few seats, and these are so arranged near the outside of the room, as to leave a large area in the centre, on the sides and in front of the stage. The wings are three stories high, and are divided into 12 mansion rooms each, and 24 bedrooms. The bedrooms are directly back of the large rooms; and the arrangement is such as to be very convenient for ventilation—a circumstance very necessary to be attended to in this warm climate.[6]

Those first months when the completed Rutledge College was pristine, must have been a pleasant time for the building committee of the Board. We can imagine their elation in viewing the tangible evidence of their stewardship. They could not know in 1805 how troublesome the presence of students was to be or that their attention was to be diverted from matters of style, taste, and siting, to the more mundane, but nonetheless pressing, matters of privies, woodlots, gardens, kitchens, fences, and all of the architectural impedimentia of the early nineteenth-century residential complex.

The first inkling of things to come arose through the need for food and discipline on campus. These two needs were immediate and demanded the construction of a Steward's Hall, or dining facility, and the provision of suitable housing for the professors. Inasmuch as the building funds had been exhausted on Rutledge and the incomplete DeSaussure, the Trustees found themselves sorely pressed, and when the inadequacy of the original appropriation became apparent, the relationship between the Board and Richard Clark began to deteriorate. Thus we find that in the final months of 1805 the Board began to question, criticize, and ultimately to disallow the invoices of their architect. In a flurry of activity at the final meetings of that year it was resolved "to urge the necessity of further appropriations for building a Steward's house on college ground and to suggest the convenience of a president's House."[7]

Even as they were seeking more capital funds, the members of the Board voted, with the other hand as it were, to demonstrate their fiscal prudence by referring a letter from their architect to the Standing Committee. This is the first instance in the relationship between the Board and Mr. Clark in which there is a suggestion of something less than immediate concordance. At the following meeting a committee was appointed to inquire into the "state of the College buildings and the sufficiency of the funds to complete them," and this committee reported in the spring of 1806, that, "having conferred with the contractor" they found that the original appropriation of $50,000 had indeed been "exhausted," that the center of DeSaussure needed to have floors and staircases installed, and finally that

> The committee will not now express an opinion upon the sufficiency of any parts of the workmanship or materials, as they are of an opinion that it will be most proper to consider that subject when the contract shall be complete, except in the plastering commenced in the Easternmost tenement of the north Edifice, which your committee on examination found so deficient as to induce them to desire the contractor to take down the whole of that which is laid upon the lathing.[8]

This committee's failure to endorse the work done on DeSaussure and their outright rejection of the wall surfaces of its "easternmost tenement" must have stirred the metabolism of Richard Clark. He had reason for concern, for from this point forward successive documents serve as milestones to mark the widening breach between the architect and the Board. Thus on 26 November 1806, Thomas Tay-

[6] Hooker, *Diary*, 852.
[7] Trustees' minutes, 16 December 1805.
[8] Ibid., 25 April 1806.

lor, as Chairman of the Standing Committee, presented his annual report to the Board.

> Early in December last, Mr. Clarke rendered in his account for extra work, many items of which, after a minute investigation and comparison with the original contract, they were of opinion ought to be paid, and others were rejected as being comprized in his contract or done without any directions from the Trustees or the Committee, which items are particularly designated in the minutes of the Committee. That part of the contract which the Committee thought proper to allow, and on the value of which they felt incompetent to decide, they agreed, at the request of Mr. Clarke, to refer to the valuation of Mr. Bennet in Charleston—but nothing more has been done on the subject.

Lacking both the contract and the minutes of the Standing Committee, we cannot know the particulars of this dispute, but the Board must have viewed it as a grave and intractable situation, for at their next meeting a discussion ensued during which the committee on the state of the College buildings reported "that they are of opinion, Mr. Clarke has failed his contracts both as to the College buildings and the Steward's house, and find upon inquiry that he makes such a variety of heavy charges on account of extra work, that they despair of ever being able to adjust his accounts by any other means than a suit at law. They therefore recommend that the Standing Committee be instructed to put his contracts in suit."[9]

After some debate the Board resolved to postpone a consideration of the above report. This matter was taken up again at the next meeting of the Board on 17 December 1806, and a lawsuit was averted only by the decision to seek authority from the legislature to employ an outside arbitrator to resolve the dispute. This solution must not have suited the architect, for on 19 December the Board discussed "a settlement between him and the said Board." At that meeting "After some debate a resolution, relative to a settlement between the Board of Trustees and Richard Clarke, the College architect, was submitted . . . but was not seconded." Unable to reach a settlement, the Board voted "that the President of the Board inform Mr. Clark, that, not being a full Board, they deem it proper to postpone the consideration of a settlement between him and the said Board until their Meeting in April."

The Board, then on motion, adjourned until the third Monday in April. This effectively left the matter in the hands of the legislature, and that body once again demonstrated its harmonious relationship with the Board:

> Reports and Resolution respecting Richard Clark
>
> In the Senate,
> December 20, 1806
>
> The Committee of the Senate, to whom was referred the resolve of the Trustees of the South Carolina College, concerning matters in dispute between them and Richard Clark, the undertaker of the college buildings, Report, That they have considered the same, and recommend that the said trustees be authorized to refer all matters in dispute between the said trustees and the said Richard Clark to indifferent and impartial persons, if the said trustees should deem it proper and expedient.
>
> Ordered, That the above resolution be sent to the House of Representatives for their concurrence.
>
> In the House of Representatives, December 20, 1806 Resolved, That this House do concur in the above resolution.[10]

[9] Ibid., 29 November 1806.
[10] Ibid., 19 December 1806. Copies of these resolutions are appended to the minutes of the Board.

The use of an arbitrator would appear to promise a felicitous solution, but in fact the subsequent history of this matter is a chronicle of frustration and delay. Time and again the settlement was postponed, either by Mr. Clark or by the Board. Then the Board rejected the arbitrator suggested by Mr. Clark and substituted John Horlbeck of Charleston. Finally they carefully drafted a procedure for the arbitration, and almost one year to the day after the first acerbic committee report concerning the work of Richard Clark, on 25 November 1807, the Minutes of the Board record that "On motion, resolved, that the secretary be requested to call on Richard Clarke, to know whether he be ready to meet Mr. Horlbeck, now in Columbia in order to take into consideration the matters in dispute between the said Richard Clarke and the Board of Trustees," and "a letter from Richard Clarke, advising the Board, that he was ready to meet the arbitrator on the part of the trustees, was then read, which was referred to the Standing Committee."

With this brief notice the first "Architect of the College Buildings" fades from view, for there is no record of the nature of the settlement, if any, in the financial statements of either Richard Clark or the College. We glimpse him obliquely once again, on 27 June 1808, when the Board "On motion Resolved that one hundred and fifty dollars be allowed Mrs. Smythe for three hundred and thirty lightwood posts used by Mr. Clarke about the College and that the treasurer be allowed to pay the same out of any monies in his hands not otherwise appropriated." Two days later Richard Clark was dead.[11]

Before the controversy surrounding the construction of DeSaussure had caused the relationship between Clark and the Trustees to become rancorous and ultimately untenable, the architect had completed Rutledge and had won both the design contest and the construction contract for the Steward's Hall, the third building erected by the South Carolina College. The legislature had appropriated $6,000 for the Steward's Hall on 20 December 1805. "The Board elected by ballot, Col. Taylor, Dr. Maxcy, Mr. Nott, Col. Hampton, Mr. Stark, a standing committee. Resolved that this standing committee choose a site and adopt a plan for a Steward's House and dining hall and contract with some person to build the same with brick materials, and that the President, when requested by the standing committee be authorized to call on the comptroller general for a warrant for monies appropriated by the Legislature to build a Stewards house." This committee elected Thomas Taylor as their chairman. They must have acted with dispatch, for at the next annual meeting, Col. Taylor reported that a

> duty assigned to the Committee was that of contracting for the building of the Steward's house. After having examined various plans presented them they adopted one proposed by Mr. Clarke, a draught of which they have ready to exhibit, and for which they agreed to give him the six thousand Dollars appropriated for that purpose. The building was to have been completed by the first of October; and was so far finished by that time as to be capable of receiving the Students, but still remains in an unfinished state. As to the execution of the work the Committee forbar to make any remarks, as the building itself affords the best evidence of the workmanship. Mr. Douglas and Mr. Yates having made proposals for building the Steward's house it was resolved that they should each be paid two Dollars for the plans proposed by them.[12]

The committee also noted that they had authorized the purchase of boilers, the construction of brick ovens, and that most of the appropriation funds had been expended. An entry in the records of

[11] The Letters of Administration for the will of Richard Clark were applied for by his widow, Elizabeth Clark on 30 June 1808. Box 5, Package 125, Richland County Probate Court Records, SCAH.

[12] Trustees' minutes, 26 November 1806.

FIGURE 25. Detail of T. Ulor painting of the South Carolina College, from the collection of the South Caroliniana Library.

the "Building Fund of the South Carolina College" in the collections of the South Carolina Department of Archives and History would appear to indicate that the final payment for the construction of the Steward's Hall was made on 23 November 1806. We know little about the internal arrangements of the Steward's Hall; however, its facade is clearly depicted in the left foreground of the Ulor painting (Figure 25) where we see that it is patterned on Rutledge. This is not surprising, for the committee in reviewing the design proposals must have considered compatibility with the existing facades as a primary desideratum. No one, of course, was more familiar with these buildings than Richard Clark. He must have confronted this design problem with confidence. His solution was to employ the same materials, to adapt the arched framing of the entry and the decorative panel in the pediment, and to use flanking wings to balance the facade. The architectural and historical significance of his solution lies in the fact that the Steward's Hall demonstrated how smaller buildings could be related harmoniously to Rutledge and DeSaussure, thus insuring the visual continuity of the Horseshoe.

The Steward's Hall was constructed in order that the students might eat on campus, and it is chiefly remembered for the complaints inevitably attendant its function. It is interesting to note that upon the completion of the Steward's Hall the Board undertook several projects to permit the president and the faculty to live in proximity to the students, an arrangement then deemed necessary for the maintenance of order. The onerous role of in loco parentis was reluctantly assumed by the faculty, many of whom protested at the prospect of living with and among the students and dining with them in the Steward's Hall. Even the patient Jonathan Maxcy, apparently in a moment of despair, after having lived on the Horseshoe for more than a decade, suggested to the Trustees the desirability of "the removal of the Presidents of the College, as soon as may be, into a house near the College."[13] However, nobody spoke of the disadvantages of free faculty housing on 19 December 1806, when the legislature in response to a request from the Board of Trustees appropriated "a sum not exceeding $8000" for the construction of a house for the president of the College. On the same day the Trustees "Resolved, that a Committee of the Board be appointed to designate and fix the style and manner in which the said house shall be finished, and of the Offices and other buildings which are to be attached to it; and that the Chairman of the Standing Committee be directed to advertize for proposals to complete the same—Dr. Maxcy, Col. Hampton and Mr. Nott, were the Committee."

Having provided a home for the president, the Board, at the same meeting "Resolved that the Standing Committee be authorized to make such arrangements in and about the College edifices as they may deem necessary for the convenient accomodation of the Professors—And that for this purpose they are to be authorized to make use of any monies in the Treasury not otherwise appropriated."

As all monies were "otherwise appropriated" this resolution proved to be an empty gesture. Several years were to pass before housing was provided for the faculty. But the plans for the president's house developed apace. On 25 February 1807,

> The Board having examined the plan for a President's house, exhibited by Messers Yates and Philips, and having agreed to adopt the outline of the same therefore Resolved, that a committee of three be appointed to designate and fix the style and manner in which the said house shall be finished, and of the Offices and other buildings which are to be

[13] A letter from Jonathan Maxcy to the Board of Trustees, transmitted to the legislature on 6 December 1820 by John Geddes, President of the Board. SCAH.

FIGURE 26.
The President's House, c. 1820, photographer unknown, from a private collection.

attached to it; and that the Chairman of the Standing Committee be directed to advertize for proposals to complete the same—Dr. Maxcy, Col. Hampton and Mr. Nott, were the Committee.

April 21, 1807 Various proposals for building a President's house were received, and refered to the following Committee. His Honor the Lieutenant Governor, Col. Taylor and Dr. Maxcy.

April 21, 1807 A letter, accompanied with Bills of Expenditure and Admeasurement from Richard Clark, was received, and ordered to lie upon the table.

April 23, 1807 The building Committee then made their report, which was as follows, "The Committee, to whom were refered the different plans exhibited to the Board of Trustees for building the President's house Report, that after examining all the plans, they recommend one given in by Capt. Wade with the alteration which appears on the face of the said plan, and also by leaving out the porticoes."

April 23, 1807 On motion resolved, that the Standing Committee be authorized to contract for the building of the President's house, agreeably to the plan reported by the building committee and that they be authorized to draw on the Comptroller for the money appropriated by the Legislature for that purpose. And be it further resolved, that the Standing Committee do give public notice in Mr. Faust's paper, at least once, that the building of the President's house will be let, on a day certain, to the lowest bidder, who shall be able to give goods and sufficient security for the performance of the contract.

It would appear that by April 1807, the Board had decided to build a president's house based upon the "outline," probably meaning the ground plan, of the plan submitted by "Messers Yates and Philips," combined with "one given in by Capt. Wade," and modified by the committee "appointed to designate and fix the style" of the building. None of these drawings has survived, nor do we have any detailed views of the structure prior to the modifications of the 1830s (Figures 26 and 27). We can only state with assurance,

FIGURE 27. The President's House, c. 1920, photographer unknown, from a private collection.

based upon an entry in the records of the "Building Fund of the South Carolina College" that sometime after the adoption of the plan, the Trustees "paid Yates & Phillips the full amount of the appr. for building the Presidents House $8000."[14]

The building of the president's house marks the appearance of housing problems as an area of perennial concern, a permanent agenda item at the meetings of the Board of Trustees. The following spring, for example, they determined that the faculty must more closely supervise the dormitory life of the students, by adopting on 27 June 1808 a resolution "that one class be located in each wing of the college in such manner as the Faculty shall direct. Resolved that one officer of the College be assigned to each wing whose duty it shall be to stay at the College during study hours and to visit each apartment of the students twice a day."

As the effectiveness of this policy hinged upon the palpable presence of the faculty, faculty housing was again discussed. However, the Board, perhaps for the sake of consistency, again deferred the allocation of specific monies for the development of faculty residences, in the vain hope that surplus funds would suffice. During the following year, the academic year of 1808–1809, a marked increase in the incidences of student disorder emphasized the inadequacies of the visitation policy. To meet this situation, the Board requested one of the professors, Paul H. Perrault, to move into rooms in DeSaussure. He balked. The ensuing discussion proved to be the catalyst which resulted in the development of housing for the faculty on the Horseshoe.

On several occasions during the spring of 1809 the Trustees considered the advisability of "requiring all of the professors to reside constantly within the College walls."[15] However, as such a measure would have forced the faculty to live in the dormitories "some doubts arose respecting the equity of such measures."[16] After much discussion the Board

> Resolved unanimously that from day after the first day of October next all the professors shall live within the College wall and board constantly in commons, presiding at the tables, and that for their accomodation the Standing Committee are directed to use a sum of money not exceeding [*blank*] thousand dollars out of the unexpended [*blank*] for repairing the college edifices, and that the Secretary transmit a copy of the foregoing resolutions to the professors.[17]

Here we see that the Trustees still hoped to provide faculty accommodations without a specific appropriation. This strategem had failed in 1806, 1807, and 1808. It was no more successful in 1809, and on 27 November 1809, the Board

> Resolved that the President of the Board of Trustees to draw up to the legislature a memorial stating the inconveniences resulting from the want of accommodation for the Professors within the walls, and requesting them to appropriate a certain sum of money for the purpose of erecting a building which would accommodate the several professors belonging to the college.

This request was successful; $8,000 was granted by the legislature for "a house or houses for the accomodation of the professors of the college."

The construction must have begun during the summer of 1810, for in April of that year we find that

> The Committee appointed to choose the most eligible site for the house of the professors reported that in their opinion the most proper situation for the said building is the lower part of the South range of the College buildings. Whereupon Resolved that the Standing Com-

[14] SCAH. Other financial records are to be found in the papers of the Treasurer's Office of the College which are in the collections of the SCL.
[15] Trustees' minutes, 7 December 1808.
[16] Idem.
[17] Ibid., 26 April 1808.

mittee cause a house consisting of two tenements to accommodate two families to be erected at a convenient distance of the west end of the South range of the College building and that the committee on this subject be directed to report a plan in conformity with this resolution at the next meeting of the board.

Resolved that the Chairman of the Standing Committee be authorised to draw on the Comptroller for the Eight thousand dollars appropriated by the Legislature at the last session for building professors Houses.[18]

There is no record of the evolution of the plan for this "tenement," nor have the building contracts survived. We have only miscellaneous receipts which indicate the chronology of the construction and a succinct entry in the Minutes of the Board on 18 December 1810 that "The grant of $8,000 for building the professors house has been paid to Messrs Yates and Philips in full for their contract for compleating the same, the vouchers for this sum have been examined by the Compt. Genl."

This double house built by "Yates and Philips" was demolished in 1854 to make way for the current President's House. However, the image of this first faculty dwelling (which seems never to have acquired a name) is preserved in the Ulor painting and, more concretely, in McCutchen House which was erected in 1813 as a duplicate of the earlier structure. No significant documents relating to the initial construction of McCutchen House are known to exist. In plan and elevation both the first faculty house and McCutchen House appear to have been modeled upon the Blacklock House which was built in Charleston in 1800. The Blacklock House, in the major elements of both its massing and its detailing, is primarily a reflection of the New England Federal Style. Consequently, viewing McCutchen House, we are in fact examining a northern product which has been filtered, modified in its passage through Charleston and into the upcountry.

The completion of the professors' houses marks the end of the initial building phase of the College. By rights these early buildings ought to have been allowed to age gracefully, to assume a patina evocative of their historical primacy. Instead, as the Board noted in 1814, the buildings quickly became "filthy and dilapidated." The Board was responsible for the rapid deterioration of the College facilities, for they had failed to develop a maintenance policy. As a result they soon found that problems of restoration and repair had superseded schemes of construction on their agendas. The first time that they made a systematic attempt to put their house in order was in 1810 when they

Resolved that the Secretary of the Board of Trustees be required to procure a book in which shall be entered all the Sums that have been appropriated by the Legislature for the several College buildings and all which Shall hereafter be made and the manner in which they have been and shall be expended and also in which shall be entered all the Items both of receipt and expenditure reported by the College Treasurer annually and that the sum of one hundred and fifty dollars be allowed to the Secretary for his increased services.[19]

The Board's concern for the physical state of the College becomes increasingly evident after 1810, and their concern was occasioned in part by student aggression vented against the buildings. For example, in the Faculty Minutes of 4 March 1808, we find that

The attention of the board was called to the case of Samuel B. Cantey of the Sophomore Class against whom were laid several charges of misdemeanor. Strong presumptive evidence of his being engaged in an assault on the windows of the Steward's House, and in the destruction of some of the furniture about the College well, on the night of the 29th ult. It also appeared that he had, within a day or two, taken

[18] Ibid., 27 April 1810.
[19] Ibid., 18 December 1810.

fish from a fish-seller, in a private manner, without liberty, and without a compensation. . . . believing him, while here, a detriment to the College, and no advantage to himself, resolved to suspend him at once.

We ought not to single out young Samuel B. Cantey, for apparently such behavior was a general thing, so much so that two months after suspending Cantey the Board resolved "If any Student shall refuse to open the door of his room when required to do it by one of the Faculty he shall be liable to suspension or expulsion—and the Faculty when they deem it necessary may break open any room in College at the expense of those who have refused admission." The brutishness implicit in this resolution is, of course, scarcely credible today. But a great deal of material documents the dire architectural consequences of student behavior during the first quarter of the nineteenth century. In this regard we need merely to glance at a faculty report on

State of the Windows of the two Center buildings of the So Carolina College and all the passages at & prior to the 5th Dec, 1812 viz

	Broken
The Chappel exclusive of the inhabited rooms	53 lights
Apparatus & Lecture rooms	16
Passage windows	36
Library	23
North Recitation Room	28
South do	36
11 by 16	
	192
Passage Windows & sides narrow	13
	205

Tenement No 2 Broken Glass 12 by 10	56
the inside frame of [*illegible*] sash wanting	
3 one sash wanting	54
4 one do	16
5	25
7	77
8 [*document deteriorated at this point*][20]	71

Here, in a partial listing taken in the dead of winter, we have a total of 504 broken windows. Nor is this inventory unique. In the following spring, a similar report concerning the chapel shows the

State of the Windows of the two Center buildings and all the Passages as taken 19th April, 1813

The Chappel exclusive of the inhabited rooms	Broken lights
in the 3rd story . . . . . . 11 by 16 . .	81
Apparatus & Lecture rooms	12
North Recitation Room . .	29
South do	28
Library	22
Over front Door	5
Window over back door	7
do 3rd story	4
do over front door 3rd story	16
narrow side sashes all gone	
	204[21]

Perhaps, in part, the dilapidated state of the College windows can be traced to the fact that the Trustees had not clearly defined in their own minds the responsibility and procedure for building maintenance. Thus, we find in 1811 that DeSaussure, one of the more active of the early Trustees, requested Thomas Park, Professor of Lan-

[20] SCL. Miscellaneous File.
[21] Idem.

guages and Treasurer of the College, to supervise some repairs, and Mr. Park refused, saying that

> The law makes it the duty of the Steward under the direction of the Committee to attend to such repairs. I would further state that the roof of the south wing leaks from end to end, that repeated attempts have been made and much money expended to render it tight to no purpose. I believe from the experiments which have been made that the Committee have long since despaired of making it tight by any other means than by taking off the slate and substituting shingles.[22]

Faced with leaking roofs and broken windows, the Board sought to remedy the situation. It is interesting to observe that only two days after the Trustees received the second report on the state of the College windows, they identified President Maxcy as their scapegoat, for at the meeting of the Board on 21 April 1813:

> The Board then went into a consideration of the state of the College, & particularly the conduct of Dr. Maxcy as relating to its government and discipline, when after mature deliberation the following resolution was adopted—viz
>
> Whereas from the communications made to the Board, and from the inspection of the Board itself, it appears that the President of the College has been guilty of many & great derelictions of duty, by which the discipline of the College has been almost totally relaxed, and this Institution is suffering severely to the injury of the Public—wherefore
>
> Resolved that the Board is deeply dissatisfied with the conduct of Dr. Maxcy, & will consider any future derelictions of duty on his part as a ground for more decisive measure in relation to him, and that a copy of this resolution be served on him. The Board then adjourned till Saturday.

In defending himself, President Maxcy declared his total innocence in an elaborate letter to the Board. In this rebuttal he does not mention the state of the College buildings. He opens saying, "I hope the Trustees will permit me to say, that to this severe accusation, the most painful occurence of my life, I am not conscious of having given just cause."[23] And at its next meeting the Secretary of the Board noted that

> A letter was received from Dr. Maxcy in response to the resolution of last Wednesday & read. . . . The subject of Dr. Maxcy's letter was then resumed, when upon debate and motion, Resolved that the letter of Dr. Maxcy be delivered to the standing committee, with instructions to inform Dr. Maxcy, that some of the instances of dereliction of duty are the following, viz.
>
> 5th He has not paid any attention to the cleanliness and decency of the appartments of the students and of the passages & entries between them, by which means the state of the College is filthy in the extreme, and in the opinion of medical gentlemen may be productive of pestilential disease.

The President was able to mollify the Board, and there is no record of administrative action taken either against him or to insure greater diligence in the maintenance of the buildings. One outcome of this unfortunate episode was a more rigorous enforcement of the rules of the institution by the faculty. Whether or not this improved decorum is problematical, but it is certain that professorial vigilance failed to prevent a concerted assault upon the buildings by the students: The great riot of 1814 may be viewed as the fruition of nine years of surreptitious window breaking. The most vivid account of this event is found in the Minutes of the Faculty:

[22] A letter from Thomas Park to the Board of Trustees, 11 December 1811. SCL. Miscellaneous File.

[23] A letter from Jonathan Maxcy to the Board of Trustees, 24 April 1813. SCL. Miscellaneous File.

The So Carolina College February 9, 1814

The Faculty were convened this morning to make inquiry into the particulars of a serious and disgraceful tumult, which occurred, last evening, among the students and within the College bounds. The circumstances appear to be as follow, That, immediately after the annunciation of the suspensions, mentioned in the minutes of the last meeting indications of a riotous disposition were seen among several of the students—that this disposition seemed to be excited and fomented by two of [*illegible*] persons, who went into the house of Professor [*illegible*] and used threats of personal violence towards him—that these indications continued throughout the whole day, and, notwithstanding a very serious and impressive admonition by the President at Evening prayers, that, just after the ringing of the seven o'clock bell, a number of the students broke out into open and formidable rebellion, trampling upon their sacred obligations to the Law and violently resisting all the efforts of the proper authority to enforce them—that a number of persons, in various disguises, having previously drunk and distributed spiritous liquors at the College well, burnt an Effigy, which was said to be intended as an insult to Professor Blackburn—that some Students, in disguise, were station as guards at the professors houses to prevent their coming out of them—that, after the burning of the Effigy, a large body, with a Drum and Fife, rushed into the Centre building of the Northern College, broke open the Library door, did great damage to the windows of the Entries, carried off the Bell and destroyed it—that, about the same time or a little before, a furious attack, with brick bats was made on the windows of Tutor Ried's room—that a similar attack was then made on the windows of Professor Blackburn's *dwelling house* to the endangering the lives of *his family*, who were *known* to be in the house and were obliged in consequence of this attack, to leave it for some time—that, although the dwelling of the other Professors were not thus assaulted, their families were greatly terrified at such a scene of savage brutality—that the windows of the College rooms of Professors Montgomery [*illegible*] were broken—that the windows of [*illegible*] apparatus room were somewhat damaged, as also those of some of the Students—that the Faculty, finding themselves unable to restore the order of the College, had recourse to the Trustees, residing in the Town, who applied to the intendant for a civil force to quell the Riot—that He, declaring there was none competent to this purpose, called out the militia of the town—that, before the arrival of this force, the Faculty, with some of the Trustees, visited the rooms and thus ascertained the names of some who were concerned in this outrageous conduct—that when the force arrived, some resistance was attempted and some of those, thus resisting, were identified—that, after all personal opposition had ceased, much grossly abusive language was used for some time by some of the students—and that, finally, it was found necessary to keep a strong guard in one of the Professor's houses during the whole night.

In recounting outbursts such as this one, previous historians of the College note by way of explanation that the student body was quite young (the freshmen entering at fourteen) and that any anecdotal history offers a distorted view of daily affairs. Without dwelling upon exceptional events, perhaps we can envision the outset of an academic day during these years, beginning with the rites of morning, the students visiting the privies located in ranges behind Rutledge and DeSaussure, and the first College well, which was in front of DeSaussure. The bell, then housed in the cupola of DeSaussure, summoned everyone to breakfast in the Steward's Hall at eight o'clock "punctually each morning." There, in several dining rooms, with the professors "presiding at table," the meal was served. The senior professor present offered grace at the beginning and at the conclusion of the meal; no student was permitted to depart prior to the concluding benediction, when the senior class rose and retired as a body with the other classes following in succession.

Mealtimes, despite the fervent prayers of the faculty, were not tranquil, and delinquency in the commons consumed an inordinate amount of faculty time. The student body stoutly maintained that the quality of the food inspired rebellion, and in 1814 a faculty investigation "respecting the commons" found that the "tea and coffee are both very unpalatable," that there were neither butter nor fresh vegetables, that the meats provided were generally salted and that these were served "without some agreeable accompaniments, such as mustard, good vinegar . . . [and] that the mode, frequently adopted, of frying pieces of the cold Bacon and beef together, does not appear to . . . be either wholsome or palatable."[24] Finally, this faculty report notes that the fare was inferior to that available in the boarding houses in Columbia, "in which houses there is only the weekly charge of three dollars, for diet, including a daily moderate allowance of spiritous liquors, with lodging. . . ." This criticism was the coup de grace, for by law these boarding houses established the benchmark of quality incumbent upon the Steward of the College.

In recalling the early dining facilities we must remember that boarding on campus was compulsory. No student, excepting those living with their families in Columbia, could attend classes without having first procured a receipt demonstrating payment of the steward's fee. As the Steward's profits were derived wholely from what he could scrimp out of these fees, the situation was not conducive to the satisfaction of the College community. Moreover, the students of the day were not characterized by quietude and docility, and harmony at meals was, no doubt, a quixotic hope. The "Dish of Trout" duel recounted by Dr. Marion Simms is evidence, in extremis, of the problem. It was the custom for the students to rush into the dining rooms at the ringing of the Steward's bell, for seizure of a platter established proprietary prerogatives. Dr. Simms recalls an incident in which two students, a Roach of Colleton County, and an Adams of Richland County, from opposite sides of the table grasped the same dish. This occasioned insults, which resulted in a pistol duel: Adams was mortally wounded; Roach, also wounded, recovered.[25]

We know more about the internal arrangements of the Steward's Hall than we do about the classrooms. We know, for example, that the Board of Trustees purchased a trunk and a horseshoe table for the room in DeSaussure which they used as a meeting place; they also acquired cabinets for the display of the mineral collection. Then too, a complete invoice survives for the first major purchase by the College of scientific equipment for the classroom in which "Natural Philosophy," physics, chemistry and mathematics were taught.[26] From this listing we can envision the shelf-lined wall of the classroom in DeSaussure and we can reconstruct many of the exercises conducted by professors. On Friday and Saturday, the students were permitted access to the library. That is, the librarian summoned each class as a body and those who wanted, or needed, books entered the room above the chapel which was "fitted up" as a library. Here silence reigned; the students came only to the librarian's desk, submitted their requests and waited while the librarian located the item and wrapped it carefully in a heavy brown paper. Students were allowed "one quarto for three weeks, or one octavo for two weeks, or two duodecimos for one week." These library hours afford us a pleasurable image of the past, of the sophomore class, for example, waiting patiently in a file winding up the stairway of Rutledge College, like supplicants approaching a sanctum.[27]

[24] A report by Professor George Blackburn, 29 April 1814. SCL. Miscellaneous File.
[25] J. Marion Sims, *The Story of My Life* (New York: D. Appleton, 1884), 89.
[26] Treasurer's Office. SCL.
[27] Frances Burnett Everhart, "The South Carolina College Library" (unpublished thesis, University of South Carolina, 1965), is a good source of information concerning the use of the library.

The Growth *of the* College

The Chemistry and Library Building, the Maxcy Monument, Pinckney and Elliott Colleges and the South Caroliniana Library

1813-1840

The architectural history of the South Carolina College is of course directly related to the growth of the College community. The Trustees, in their original advertisements had stipulated that the initial building should be "calculated as to be capable of accomodating the greatest possible number of students." When the College opened in 1805 with nine students, a president and one faculty member, there was little pressure for further construction. The second building, DeSaussure, was begun in 1806, but progressed slowly by fits and starts until November 1807 when a committee of the Board reported that "from the number of Students at this time in the South Carolina College and the probable increase of numbers in the course of the ensuing year your committee are of opinion that it becomes also immediately necessary to finish the centre building of the Northern range of the College for the reception of students."[1]

The building appears to have been fully occupied the following year. A Steward's Hall and houses for the President and faculty comprised the facilities prior to 1815, when the enrollment had grown to more than 200 students. In 1815 the only classrooms were those in the central blocks of Rutledge and DeSaussure, and in that year the faculty began to request that additional space be developed for academic use. Surviving documents suggest that the Rev. Christian Hanckel, a tutor of Mathematics, and Dr. Edward Darrell Smith, Professor of Chemistry and Mineralogy, provided the impetus for the development of the first building on the campus devoted entirely to academic use. Their requests are stated in a letter written by William DeSaussure, as secretary to the Board, to Governor David R. Williams on 19 November 1815:

> I have the honor to communicate to your Excellency the following extract from the report of the Standing Committee of the Board of Trustees. The Committee further submit several communications from the Revd. Tutor Mr. Henkle and Professor Smith. They both report that the room appropriated to the safe keeping of the Philosophical Instruments and Chemical Apparatus is too small, and prevents their being kept in good order—and that some of the instruments suffer

[1] Trustees' minutes, 30 November 1807.

materially from their exposure to the corroding and noxious gases used in the Chemical experiments. And professor Smith complains that the room is extremely inconvenient for the attendance of the students on his lectures. The Committee are satisfied of the truth of these representations, and beg leave to represent that a separate building of brick, made fire proof, is necessary to the perfection of this part of the system. A brick building might be constructed which would answer the purposes of an apparatus room, lecture rooms for the chemical and mathematical Professors, and a library room, with an observatory and a considerable annual expence might be saved on the insurance of the Library and apparatus. But the expence could not be defrayed without the aid of the Legislature. The Committee therefore recommend that an application be made to the Legislature for that purpose.

And thereupon it was resolved by an unanimous vote of the Board of Trustees that his Excellency the Governor and President of the Board be requested to make a communication to the Legislature recommending that the above measure be carried into effect.

Here we find that the Trustees concurred with the faculty's desire to expand the space allotted to the library and to the sciences; parenthetically we should note that the earliest surviving statement concerning the desirability of an observatory is found in this committee report. In addition to these materials we have a schematic ground plan of the proposed structure (Figure 28). This plan presents the configuration of the building and labels the intended uses of the various rooms: the first level is earmarked as the domain of Dr. Smith and Rev. Hanckel; the Rev. Hanckel is also assigned one quarter of the second story. Unfortunately this plan is not signed, nor is the cryptic explanation, or caption, which accompanied it. Both items have survived inside a packet of legislative materials on which is jotted "1815 Enclosing two letters from Dr Smith and Rev Hankle respecting the Philosophical and Chemical Apparatus."[2]

[2] SCAH. South Carolina College materials in the Green Files.

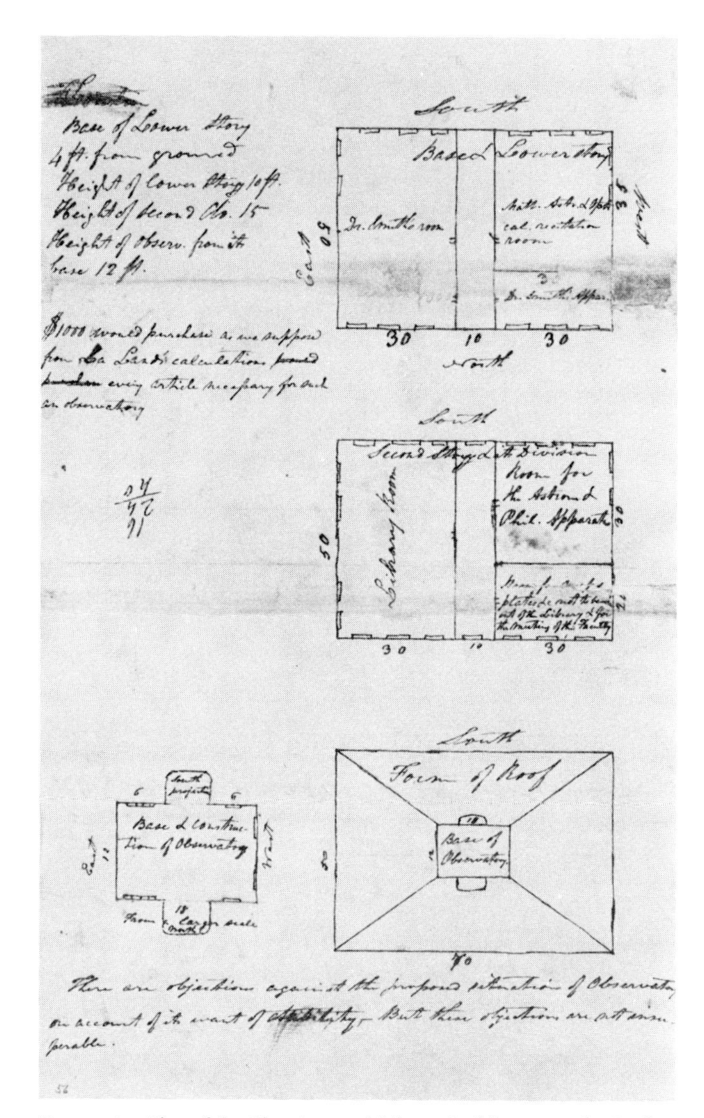

FIGURE 28. Plan of the Chemistry and Library Building, 1815, by Professors Christian Hanckel and Edward Darrell Smith, from the collection of the South Carolina Department of Archives and History.

We might assume then, that Smith and Hanckel drafted the plan and its "caption," which says:

> The expence of Building a House 75 by 53 feet 2 Story high each of 15 feet pitch The Base or Foundation to be 4 feet above the ground The Wall of it to be 2½ Bricks The Lower Story to be 2 do thick The Second to be 1½ do The 2 middle partitions to be 1½ do The observatory 18 by 12 Height 12 feet with 2 projections of 5 feet to shew a half octagon with an inside finish equal to the other Buildings of the College 42 Windows of 18 Lights of glass 10 by 12 will cost \$9500.[3]

Two elements of this design proposal are noteworthy. First, there is an attempt to make the building more resistant to fire through the use of brick interior partitions. (The Board of Trustees made much of this fact when they requested the necessary funds to begin construction.) Secondly, the observatory perched upon the peak of the hipped roof represented an elaboration of the then existing cupolas on Rutledge and DeSaussure. This cupola observatory, if built, would have been impressive.

The legislature was impressed by the proposal, but not enough to appropriate the \$9,500 estimated necessary by the creators of the plan. In 1815 the legislature approved an expenditure of \$6,000 for the new building, and soon thereafter DeSaussure, as chairman of the building committee, wrote to the Board that:

> The committee appointed to make a contract for the erection of new brick building in the College yard for the use of the institution
>
> Report that they made a contract with Zachariah Phillips who offered to furnish the materials & erect the building at a much lower price than was offered by any other workman. The contract is now laid before the board—by it he engaged to find all the materials, & to furnish the building according to the plan of the professors at six thousand one hundred dollars. The observatory however was not included in this contract, because the plan was not then fixed on by the faculty & it being an unusual work here, a correct estimate could not be furnished. It has since been constructed & the whole exterior of the building is nearly completed.
>
> Mr. Philips has since furnished an estimate for erecting the observatory, for removing & re-erecting the library shelves, for fitting up the Laboratory & apparatus rooms & for all such parts of the inside work as were not comprehended in the original contract. It amounts to the large sum of nearly eighteen hundred dollars. The Legislature doubtless intended to compleat the building, but as no precise estimate of the expence could then be furnished an appropriation of no more than six-thousand dollars was made. It will now therefore be necessary than [*sic*] application be made for a new appropriation of two thousand dollars to cover the deficiency.
>
> The new building being constructed entirely fire proof will become the depository of the Library as well as of the philosophical & astronomical apparatus which are of great value. And it will supercede the necessity of insurance on those objects, which will be a considerable annual saving. The old Library room may be converted as well as the old apparatus & lecturing rooms into lodging rooms, and will accomodate at least ten students
>
> Henry W Desaussure, Chairman of the Building Committee[4]

It must have been true, as DeSaussure suggests, that the "Legislature doubtless intended to complete the building" with the initial appropriation of \$6,000, but that did not happen. The Board initiated the project by drafting a contract which did not entail either the observatory or the interior finishing of the classrooms, the offices, or the library. There is no record of the political minuet by which the Trustees obtained—without censure—the monies needed to finish the building in 1817.

The completed Library and Science building (it was never dignified with any other name) appears in the right hand foreground of

[3] Idem.
[4] Idem. An undated manuscript copy of DeSaussure's letter.

FIGURE 29. "View of the North side of the South Carolina College building during the presence of a double rainbow of a perfect segment located as represented above. July 10, 1823. Columbia," by Robert Mills, from the collection of Tulane University.

the Ulor painting, and here we see that its exterior treatment closely resembled McCutchen House. Thus the Library and Science building, a red brick facade with decorative panels, white trim and deep green shutters, sited across the mall from the Steward's Hall, continued the mirror-image tradition which had begun with Rutledge and DeSaussure. The observatory was not located upon the Horseshoe; instead it was erected as a separate building behind McCutchen or DeSaussure, and we know it today only as a dome visible in the extreme left-hand corner of the Ulor painting, or as a few lines in the "Rainbow Drawing" by Robert Mills (Figure 29). These small images appear to be the only surviving records of the existence of this observatory.

The observatory and the Library and Science building were the last to be erected during the tenure of Jonathan Maxcy as President of the South Carolina College. He died in office on 4 June 1820. With justice his memorial might have borrowed the inscription which is found upon the tomb of Sir Christopher Wren, "*Si monumentum requiris, circumspice.*" President Maxcy, through an effective relationship with the Trustees and the legislature had presided over sixteen years of sustained growth and development, formative years which established the architectural character of the College. We can bring the importance of his leadership into sharper focus if we compare the development during his presidency with the work accomplished by his successor. We need only to observe that after the death of Dr. Maxcy, fully fifteen years passed before the legislature again appropriated any significant funds for the College buildings. During the years 1820–1834 the face of the College mellowed undisturbed: appropriately, the only obvious change during this period was the placement in the center of the mall of a monument to the memory of Dr. Maxcy.

The Maxcy Monument (Figure 30) was erected by the Clariosophic Society in 1827, and it is significant beyond its memorial intent or its visual prominence. Much of the anecdotal history of the College pivots about its base. Here, for example, the student body prior to 1836 periodically piled the wooden steps and porches of the college buildings to fuel fires in the night. The vitality of the Clariosophic Society is made concrete in the monument: with impressive persistence the student members of the society hounded their alumni and their honorary membership for contributions to complete the structure.

It is in the manuscript records of the Clariosophic Society that we can trace the development of the Maxcy Monument. The survival of these materials is most fortunate inasmuch as the participation of Robert Mills—at a critical moment in his own development—lends national significance to this work. Immediately prior to the death of Dr. Maxcy, Robert Mills had been residing in Baltimore, where he was directing the construction of the monument which he had designed in 1814 to the memory of George Washington. In 1820 a lack of funds brought the work in Baltimore to a halt, and Mills moved his family to Columbia in order to accept a position on the South Carolina Board of Public Works. Although Mills came to reside in Columbia in the year of Dr. Maxcy's death, there is no evidence to suggest that the monument project was considered prior to February 1824. It is true that the Society had, on 10 June 1820, inserted in their minutes a *Momento Moria*, a notice of Dr. Maxcy's demise, and they did it again several years later, voting on 15 November 1823 that "The Clariosophic society desireous of testifying their regard for the memory of Mr Jonathan Maxcy, and of paying a last tribute of respect to a deceased friend & brother, hence ordered that his death be inserted in the records of the society."[5] In the interim—between 1820 and 1823—there is no indication that plans for the monument were under way.

[5] Clariosophic Society minutes, SCL.

FIGURE 30. The Maxcy Monument, from a photograph by Judith Steinhauser.

The second notice must have coincided with the outset of discussion concerning the project, for soon after the Christmas vacation of 1823, we find a cryptic entry in the minutes of the society meeting of 21 February 1824 directing "That: a committee of three be appointed to wait on Colonel Gregg and obtain leave to erect the monument on Dr Maxcy's grave. The committee consisted of Messs Kennedy Jones & Calhoun." And within the week, on 28 February 1824, we find that "The president then read the following letter, received from George McDuffie, addressed to Mr. James M. Daniel President, Clariosophic Society:"

> Washington Febry 15, 1824
>
> Sir
>
> I am much gratified by the information, that the Clariosophic Society has collected a sum sufficient to erect a monument (illustrative of the gratitude of its members) to the memory of our common benefactor Dr. Maxcy; and it will give me pleasure to make arrangements for the judicious appropriation of the fund, by securing the services of a skilful artist. If it is expected that I shall write the epitaph, I would thank you to ascertain and inform me the age of Dr Maxcy and the day of his death.
>
> Your Obdt. Ser.
> Geo. McDuffie[6]

From this letter, we might assume that George McDuffie, then a distinguished congressman from South Carolina, set about to "secure the services of a skilful artist" in February 1824. However, it would appear that McDuffie left this to Mr. William K. Clowney, a tutor of Mathematics at the College, for on 12 May 1824, Mr. Clowney wrote to Charles R. Carroll, who was then President of the Society:

[6] Idem.

Dear Sir,

In compliance with the resolution of the Clariosophic Society requiring me to state "what progress has made in procuring the monument of Revd Dr. Maxcy and when the work is likely to be completed" I beg leave through you to make the following report—

Since the money intended to defray the expenses of the monument has been deposited in my hands I have made every exertion in my power to have the work speedily executed. I am sorry, however, because of the absences of the Hon. George McDuffie from the state, who shares equally with me the importent trust confided, that the progress of the work is not equal to my wishes, nor perhaps to your expectations. Soon after the money had been placed in my hands, with the assistance of Mr. Mills a *plan* for the monument was devised, which *plan* I immediately transmitted to the Hon. George McDuffie at the city of Washington for his opinion, together with some reasons why I thought it best to have the work executed in Carolina marble by the artists of Columbia. In answer to this letter Mr McDuffie writes on the 20th of March 1824 in these words "I have delayed answering your letter in the hope of having it in my power to consult an able artist on the subject of the monument. Having been disappointed, I have to say that the plan you enclosed seems to me to be a very good one, and the best we can do will probably be to have it executed as you propose. If I should have it in my power in a short time (as I probably shall) to consult an artist of distinguished genius I shall communicate the result." This is the only communication I have received from Mr McDuffie relative to the subject, and thus far we may be said to have acted together. But encouraged by the tenor of Mr McDuffie's letter, & the generous offer of Col. Nesbit to gratuitously bestow us the marble also satisfied as to the taste & skill of the Columbia artists as well as the reasonableness of their charge, & assured at the same time by Mr Mills an able judge of all such matters that he would personally attend to its proper execution I have gone so far as partially to engage the Columbia artists to make & erect the monument, provided our marble can be obtained suitable to our purpose. In consequence of this arrangement (in which I have not failed to consult economy, expedition & the ablest workmanship) one of the artists is now employed in examining the quarry & should he succeed in obtaining sufficient quantity of white marble for our purpose the work will probably be completed in the course of the summer.

With sentiments of the highest esteem I remain

William K Clowney[7]

From this we learn that Mills drafted his plan, which was apparently accepted without modification, prior to the middle of March 1824. We note furthermore that Mr. Clowney, "encouraged by the tenor of Mr. McDuffie's letter," began to "partially engage the Columbia artists to make & erect the monument" before the middle of May. At this point the project became dormant for some five months. The following fall the minutes of the Society record that "On the evening of October 9, 1824, 'after the election of Mr. R. Mills to an honorary membership' the Society elected its officers, choosing John L Kennedy of the monument committee as vice president."

During Mr. Kennedy's tenure in office the Society debated, as was its custom, the great questions of the day, but the matter of the monument was also pressed forward. On the evening of 10 December 1825, for example, following a heated discussion on the topic "Do males or females enjoy most happiness?" the minutes show that the following report was made:

> The committee on "the monument" beg leave to report that immediately after their appointment in June last in accordance with the resolution then passed, they waited on Mr. Mills acting architect, and informed him to their consideration, & requested him to enter into a contract with suitable persons for the performance of the business. They likewise requested his acceptance of the appointment of adjunct commissioner with Messers Clowney & McDuffie in the management of the undertaking.

[7] Idem.

CIRCULAR.

Clariosophic Hall, *February* 1826.

To the Honorary Members of the Clariosophic Society of the South-Carolina College.

THE CLARIOSOPHIC SOCIETY, *anxious to testify its gratitude and respect to the memory of* Dr. MAXCY, *have adopted a more enlarged plan, proposed by* Mr. R. MILLS, (Engineer and Architect,) *for his Monument, than the one previously contemplated.*

In the execution of this plan, it has become necessary to appeal to the liberality of its Honorary Members: we, therefore, (a Committee appointed to superintend the Monument,) have been empowered to address circulars soliciting their contributions. It is to be erected in the College Campus, and the corner-stone has already been laid. We have received considerable sums from some members. A workman has been engaged—the materials have been received, and the whole can be completed in two months from this time. Its cost is estimated at one thousand dollars. We would now invite your particular attention to this subject, and we fondly hope our expectations may be realized.

The Committee, and persons appointed by it, will receive subscriptions in the districts in which they respectively reside.

Your's, with the highest respect,

JOHN K. CHARLES,
DANIEL S. HENDERSON,
FRANCIS W. PICKENS, } *Committee.*

Description

OF THE

MONUMENT TO BE ERECTED IN THE CAMPUS

OF THE

SOUTH-CAROLINA COLLEGE,

TO THE MEMORY OF

DR. MAXCY,

FIRST PRESIDENT OF THE SAME,

BY THE

CLARIOSOPHIC SOCIETY.

THE Design embraces the idea of a frustrum of a column elevated on its pedestal, and based on a solid square zocle; the whole surmounted by the classic symbol of immortality, the Tripod.

The *zocle*, which rises about nine feet, is a perfect cube, of granite. The *superstructure*, (pedestal and frustrum of the column) is of marble. The tripod is of metal bronzed.

On each face of the granite zocle is inserted a marble tablet for inscriptions.

The pedestal of the column presents on every face of the Die, the diamond key tablet of the Society, for its insigna, and such other inscriptions as may be necessary. This die is crowned by the peculiar monumental cap, ornamented at each angle with the honey suckle quadrants.

The frustrum of the surmounting column is divided in its heighth into three parts, the centre is a square projecting block, with a star on each face, symbolical of the merit of the deceased. The whole structure to be elevated about twenty-five feet, and enclosed by an iron railing.

FIGURE 31. The Circular of the Maxcy Monument Committee, from the collection of the South Caroliniana Library.

Your committee at the same time addressed circulers, & the plan laid down by the resolutions, to all the honorary members of the Clariosophic Society requesting their assistance in the undertaking.[8]

The circular (Figure 31) distributed by the committee described the plan by Robert Mills in language which would have daunted all but the most ardent student of the architectural revival styles—The circular spoke of the "frustrum of a column," of the "zocle," "tripod," and the "Die."

The Monument Committee, having solicited support and circulated their plan, reported further on 10 December 1825:

When your committee returned after Summer vacation, they made enquiries into the result of these two proceedings. They were glad to find that Mr Mills had entered into the following contract with Mr. Brown.

Articles of *agreements*

Whereas the Clariosophic Society of the So Carolina College intend to erect a monument, in the town of Columbia So Carolina, to the memory of Dr. Maxcy, agreeably to the design of Robert Mills architect, hereunto annexed, & whereas, Mr. Brown stone cutter of the town of Columbia aforesaid, is willing & doth hereby agree to execute the said work in marble, & granite in the best & most workman-like manner, & agreeable to the design of the said Robert Mills, & under his direction. Now therefore it is agreed between the same parties in form & manner following. That is to say first, on the part of the said Clariosophic Society by their committee signing this contract for the said society, they agree for, & in consideration of the work hereafter to be specified being done in a faithful & workman-like manner, & according completion of the same, the sum of eight hundred seventy three Dollars (not including the tripod which will be of metal) Should any payment be received during the progress of the work, the same may be made by the committee at their option. And on the part of the

[8] Idem.

said Wm Brown, he covenants & agrees, in consideration of the above compensation, being or to be made to him on the completion of the said work, agreeably to the design of the said Robert Mills, & the specifications annexed & signed by the parties (And which form part of the agreement) he shall & will at his *own* proper cost, & expence of labour, & all materials erect the said monument in the town of Columbia in such place as may be fixed upon by the said Committee, executing the work in the best & most faithful manner, & with the best quality of materials, having the said work ready to put up in all the month of November next, & have the same finished in one month after, if required by the said Committee.

And for the true & faithful performance of all & singular the articles & covenants herein specified, the undersigned bind themselves their heirs & successors, this 7th day of July in the year of our Lord one thousand eight hundred & twenty five.

(signed) Robert Mills—for the committee of the Clariosophic Society—

Witnessed by

William Brown[9]

W. N. C. Lusser . —

This document, signed by Robert Mills and William Brown, makes it clear that Mills, beyond designing the monument, drafted the necessary specifications and contract and that he, as an "adjunct commissioner" for the society, personally saw that the work was carried out "under his direction." With a design in hand and a campaign for funds under way, the Society laid the cornerstone of the Monument with much ado early in December 1825. In preparation for the ceremony, the Clariosophic Society had debated whether or not to invite the other literary organization, the Euphradian Society, to participate in the procession. At a special meeting held on 13 December such an invitation was "almost unanimously rejected." The following evening, as the debate raged on, charity prevailed, and the invitation was extended. The Euphradians, however, declined to participate, and their letter of refusal evokes the sense of propriety then prevalent among the student body:

Euphraidian Hall, S C College, 16 Decr 1825

Gentlemen of the Clariosophic Society,

Our Society received with respect your communication inviting us to join you in laying the corner stone of your monument to Dr Maxcy, & having considered it with that politeness, with which we always regard communications from your body, deem it best to decline the honor which you have profferred us—the number of our members being much lessened at the present time & several of our principal officers being absent would prevent us from appearing in such a manner as either to gratify you or do honor to the occasion. You may imagine [*illegible*] that we should feel a great delicacy in sharing the honors without dividing with you the expense. Had we combined our efforts with you in erecting this monument to one, whose memory we all respect so highly & whose loss we so much regret nothing could have afforded us so much pleasure as to participate with you in a ceremony so solemn & important—From these considerations, Gentlemen, the Society have thought proper to decline your invitation & have appointed us to communicate the resolution

Yours respectfully,

Silas L. Heller
H. W. Hilliard
Edmund Bellinger[10]

Without the direct support of the student body as a whole, the Clariosophic Society pressed on to raise the money to erect the monument. Although the design had been prepared by 1 March 1824, several years elapsed before the final construction began. On 17 March 1827, the Clariosophic Society determined that sufficient monies were on hand to complete the work and that:

[9] Idem.
[10] Idem.

We would also mention that Professor Henry has the inscription ready & that Mr. Mills the architect expects the tripod soon & that the workman know the materials necessary. So that we are perfect confident the whole can by proper management be finished in a few weeks. We would recommend that it be nicely finished off and that a neat railing be constructed to inclose it. We would also recomend that the conclusion of these transactions be taken down in writing & properly atested. We would also state that if any mismanagement should turn out with Mr. Mills that it will be the mismanagement of the first committee that was appointed as their arrangement with him could not be altered by any of their successors. All of which is submited to your consideration at the same time perfectly satisfied as we are, that the work will be an ornament to the campus and an honor to the beloved society the recollection of which it shall ever be our pride to cherish with proudest & dearest feelings

T W Pickens
Chairman of the Committee on the Monument[11]

Following the acceptance of this report another monument committee was elected, and in due time they reported that:

The committee on the Monument pursuant to custom, beg leave to make the following report That since their appointment to superintend the progress of the monument they have been unremitting in their exertions to forward the work that they have for that purpose made frequent calls on Mr. Mills to ascertain the state of the business that after much disappointment they have in the late arrival of the [*illegible*] been induced to hope the completion of the monument is at no distant period. Your committee feel much pleasure in stating that the inscription has for some time past been in readiness that the workmen are in waiting to pursue the farther directions of Mr. Mills who is at present at the north and said to be expected after the first fall of Frost. As your Committee entertain some apprehension concerning the certainty of Mr Mills return they could solicit a continuance in office if the Society shall approve the same until the eighteenth of December inasmuch as the management and direction of the Monument has been carried on by Mr. Mills—if however he does not return at that time your committee will then be furnished with such positive intelligence as will enable the Society to act with more certainty and greater efficiency. Your committee beg leave farther to report the state of the funds with regard to the monument: paid by a former Committee to Mills three hundred dollars. Paid Brown by a former committee one hundred dollars.[12]

In the fall of 1827 Robert Mills must have returned to Columbia "after the fall of the first Frost" and tended to the construction of the monument. On 15 December 1827, with a Masonic ritual, the Maxcy Monument was dedicated with Robert Mills in attendance.

The Maxcy Monument is a notable milestone in the history of American design. Having been conceived in the spring of 1824 and begun during the summer of 1825, it represents an early example of the Egyptian Revival Style. More importantly perhaps, the monument appears to have been the earliest use of this style by Robert Mills; consequently, the Maxcy Monument stands at the outset of a personal development which culminated in 1836 with the design of Robert Mills' masterpiece, the Washington Monument in Washington, D.C. Mills' interest in Egyptian forms antedated the South Carolina College project. Indeed, in 1820, before returning to South Carolina, he had composed an extensive and thoroughly researched "Essay on Architectural Monuments" for the *Analectic Magazine* of Philadelphia. Here he had written that "to cherish the recollection of those who have lived an ornament and benefit to the world . . . is not only a duty we owe to their memory, but an advantage to ourselves."[13] He reviewed at length the funerary customs of the Egyptians, and then, speaking specifically of their obelisks, said:

[11] Idem.
[12] Idem.
[13] Robert Mills, "Essay on Architectural Monuments," *The Analectic Magazine*, Vol. I, No. IV (April, 1820), 277–78.

> Of all the works of the Egyptians, there are none more remarkable than the obelisks, which have excited the admiration of travellers, and the wonder of the philosopher and the naturalist—They were pyramidal spires, composed of one entire stone, cut with hieroglyphics, and erected to convey to posterity the fame and power of their founders—Sesostris, who reigned 3300 years since, raised two, each of which was of one piece of granite, 180 feet high; the side of the square base 30 feet; one of these was transported to Rome by Augustus, and placed in the Campus Martius. The son of Sesostris raised one which was taken to Rome by Caligula. But none of these were equal in size to that erected near Heliopolis by Ramesses, who reigned 3000 years since; it is the most valuable monument which now remains of Egyptian antiquity. It was respected by Cambyses when he put all to fire and sword, ordering the flames of the city to be extenguished, when he saw them approaching the obelisk—Constantine transported it to Rome and placed it in the circus, it there fell and was broken, but the care of pope Sixtus V, repaired and restored it.[14]

Mills' awareness of Egyptian forms no doubt stemmed from French publications. The volume, for example, *Lubersac sur les monumens publiques* published in Paris in 1775, was available to Mills in the library of Thomas Jefferson and illustrates the author's proposal for a grandiose obelisk commemorating the family of Louis XVI. And Vivant Denon's *Voyage dans la basse et la haute Egypte* published in Paris in 1802 contains an illustration of the lower portion of a pylon at Apollinopolis Parva, an illustration which is strikingly similar to both the base and to the cavetto molding of the Maxcy Monument; indeed, the similarity extends even to the ashlar pattern of the granite and to the use of the winged disc—emblematic of eternity—upon the molding. Denon's *Voyage* enjoyed a wide circulation, and three English editions of this work were reviewed by the Baltimore *Observer* of 10 October 1807, where "the book was pronounced the most important work issuing from the Egyptian expedition." Quite probably Mills knew this work and specifically used Denon's drawing of the pylon at Apollinopolis Parva in developing the Maxcy Monument.

In reviewing Mills' work we are struck time and again by the evidences of his omniverous reading habits. His studies kept him abreast of technological and stylistic changes. The Egyptian Revival elements of the Maxcy Monument demonstrate his position among the avant-garde of the 1820s. Motifs, for example, such as the winged disc seldom appeared in America prior to 1824, but after that date this device was used extensively. Mills continued to employ Egyptoid forms in his own work, thus his DeKalb Monument (Figure 32) in Camden, South Carolina (1825), and the Clinton Memorial in Alexandria, Virginia (1841), are conceptually akin to the Maxcy Monument. He did not, however, restrict his use of the Egyptian Revival vocabulary to small, personal memorials. Thus when he was invited by the Bunker Hill Monument Association to submit a proposal in the competition for the design of a memorial, he wrote on 20 March 1825:

> I have the honor to submit for your consideration and approval, a design for the monument you propose erecting on the spot, where the brave General Warren and his worthy associates fell: to commemorate their valor, and the gratitude of their country. . . . To the subject of monuments, I have for many years devoted my attention, and studied the character and design of the most eminent of these structures, ancient and modern, extant, with a view to offer to my countrymen the result of my professional labors when called upon to do so. The genius of our people and government, in all their national works, embraces greatness of outline: and it remains for those who have the formation of the designs to endeavor to combine in them, economy with good taste—simplicity, I have always considered as the ground work of beauty and good taste, in all things. To [this] rule I have endeavored to conform in all my designs, in the design for the monu-

[14] Ibid., 281.

FIGURE 32 *left.* The DeKalb Monument, Camden, South Carolina, 1825, by Robert Mills, from a photograph by Robert M. Smith, Photo-Vision, Columbia.

FIGURE 33 *above.* The Bunker Hill Monument, 1825, from a lithograph drawn by A. J. Davis and published by Pendleton's Lithography.

> ment which I now have the honor to lay before you, I would recommend the adoption of the obelisk form, in preference to the column —the detail I have affixed to the species of pillar, will be found to give it a peculiarly interesting character, embracing originality of effect with simplicity of design, economy in execution, great solidity and capacity for decoration, reaching to the highest degree of splendor consistent with good taste.[15]

Following the submission of this letter, which was accompanied by a model and a painting of the proposed granite shaft, Mills heard no more from the Commission. We can imagine his chagrin when he learned that they had determined to erect an obelisk of the proportions presented in his design (Figure 33). He asked a lawyer to investigate the matter for him. The question of authorship was not resolved by Mills' attorney and to this day it remains unsettled. For our purposes, it is enough to note that Mills' proposal itself is further evidence of his interest in large, simple Egyptoid forms. Moreover, this proposal, like his more modest monuments, must be viewed primarily as a prelude to his crowning achievement, the designing in 1836 of the Washington Monument in the federal capital. His proposal for the Washington Monument consisted of an obelisk rising out of a round Doric temple, replete with the appropriate inscriptions, a replica of the horses of St. Mark's and a tripod (Figure 34). Financial constraints precluded the temple base, but until 1884 the shaft was entered through two Egyptian doorways surmounted by cavetto cornices upon which were carved the winged disc and the initial of the first president.

There is no record to indicate that Thomas Cooper, who succeeded Jonathan Maxcy as President of the College, participated in any way in the development of the Maxcy Monument. Indeed, Cooper showed little interest in the architecture of the College during his term as President (1821–1834). His lack of interest is reflected in the minimal appropriations made by the legislature for capital improvements during his tenure. No new construction was undertaken during his administration, and only modest amounts of money were requested or set aside for repair and maintenance of the College buildings. The average annual appropriation for the College under his administration was $15,000—it remained precisely $14,420 during the last five years he held office. But when he left office in 1834 the appropriation was increased immediately to $36,000, $20,000 of which was for "Repairing College Buildings." The following year $10,000 was appropriated "for building two Houses for the Professors" and then in 1836 "for College Buildings forty five thousand dollars for Repairs to same Buildings Ten thousand dollars." The failure of the legislature to commit substantial sums of money to construction during Cooper's administration is partially explained by the declining enrollments during this period. Dr. Daniel Walker Hollis, author of *University of South Carolina*, Volume I: *South Carolina College*, has said of these years:

> One reason the college needed no new buildings lay in the fact that the enrollment changed little and showed a slight decrease. While there were over a hundred students on the campus each year during the last ten years of Maxcy's regime, the number dropped to eighty-eight in 1821, seventy-six in 1822, and to a low of sixty-five in 1823. From 1824 to 1827 there were about 110 students per year, but in 1829 the figure dropped to eighty-seven. The years 1830 to 1832 saw enrollment reach its peak, with 115 students present in 1830. The impact of the opposition Cooper had aroused began to be felt in 1833, when only eighty-six students enrolled, and in 1834 this number declined to fifty-two.[16]

Another historian of the College, Maximillian LaBorde, acerbically notes that it

[15] Helen Mar Pierce Gallagher, *Robert Mills, Architect of the Washington Monument, 1781–1855* (New York: Columbia University Press, 1935), 204–7.
[16] Hollis, *South Carolina College*, 93–94.

FIGURE 34. The Washington Monument Proposal, 1836, by Robert Mills, from the collection of the South Caroliniana Library.

is not to be disguised, that the close of the year 1834 found the College in a deplorable condition. It was almost deserted. . . . At no period during the year did the number [of students] exceed fifty-two. Of these one was suspended and reported for expulsion, and nine took dismissals. Twenty-two had passed their final examination . . . and the whole number left in the College [at the end of the year] was twenty only. The condition of things was truly bad, and the prospect not at all encouraging. Dr. Henry reports four as having been received for the class of 1835, and his conjectural estimates only deepen the shade which rests upon the College.[17]

President Cooper might be held responsible in large measure for these declining enrollments. His reputation throughout the state as an agnostic and as a political radical caused many parents to keep their sons at home or to send them elsewhere for their education. His successful efforts to raise the minimum age for admission, from fourteen to fifteen, and to enforce rigorous entrance requirements turned away many potential students; indeed, these two policies caused there to be no freshman class and only a few sophomores in 1831. In dealing with those students on campus, Thomas Cooper's administration is notable for its extensive use of expulsion.

In 1827, when many students formed a "combination" and refused to eat in the Steward's Hall, the administration viewed it as the "Great Biscuit Rebellion," suspended seventy-five and ultimately expelled forty-one, leaving a senior class of thirteen in 1828. In these circumstances there was little need for enlarged facilities.

President Cooper's responsibility for the declining enrollments and the subsequent lack of development does not adequately portray the impact of his tenure upon the architecture of the College. Under his care, the buildings were allowed to fall into a state of dis-

[17] Maximilian LaBorde, *History of the South Carolina College* (Columbia: Peter B. Glass, 1859), 189.

repair. In suggesting that the President of the College was responsible for the deterioration of the buildings, we should note that earlier, in 1813, the Board of Trustees had specifically directed Jonathan Maxcy to tend to the maintenance of the facilities; moreover, the Board apparently deemed this system to be adequate as they did not act upon the request of the faculty in 1823 that a building supervisor be retained. Whatever the cause of the hiatus of construction and maintenance, its effect was dramatic. At the outset of the presidency of Robert Woodward Barnwell the state of the College buildings demanded attention and the resulting renovations, alterations, and additions transformed the appearance of the campus.

The resignation of Thomas Cooper was effective on 1 January 1834. During the months that followed the Committee on College Repairs acted with unwonted alacrity, with a dispatch which enabled them on 9 December 1835 to submit the following report:

> Early in the spring they made contracts for comprehensive repairs of the college edifices—Under these contracts the whole exterior of both the colleges have been painted and penciled, and the cornices repaired; and the buildings now present a fresh and new appearance. The committee believe that this work is very durable, and will not require to be renewed for many years. They found the interior of the two colleges in a deplorable state of filth and dilapidation. They caused all the rooms to be thoroughly cleansed, painted and whitewashed, and the plaistering and wood work repaired whereever it was necessary, and a cupola rebuilt upon the North College from which it had been pulled down. They caused the back doors and entry windows of the several tenements to be bricked up, and an entire reglazing of the whole college to be effected.
>
> The steps of the colleges have heretofore been of wood and have often been burnt down by the students, to the great peril of the colleges. The committee have caused these to be replaced by granite steps. Considerable repairs were found necessary in the steward's house and premises; these have been effected; and also some small repairs upon the houses of the Professors.
>
> The air of dilapidation and decay which the ragged wooden fences about the colleges always presented induced the committee to make contracts for a brick wall to surround the whole college premises, of about 6 feet 9 inches in height and such thickness as would ensure durability. This wall is in process but is not completed.
>
> As a great quantity of lime was necessary for this and other work about the college, the committee made contracts in Charleston at an early period & upon advantageous terms for a large supply of the indispensable article. A considerable portion of this was lost by the lime taking fire, and destroying the boat and the whole cargo; but the committee had taken the precaution to ensure the lime, and they have been fully re-embursed for the loss, which nevertheless occasioned some delay in their operations.
>
> In effecting these repairs the committee have expended fourteen thousand, two hundred and fifty nine dollars and fifty two cents of the sum of $200,000 [*sic*, this sum should be $20,000] This appropriated by the Legislature—and they submit herewith an account of the said expenditure accompanied by the vouchers.
>
> The whole repairs effected and those which remain to be done under the contracts entered into by the committee will be paid for by the fund appropriated, and a balance of more than one thousand dollars will probably be left until the work is completed, and the various accounts [*illegible*] the committee cannot report with certainty upon this point.
>
> The building which contains the Library requires repairs; the centre partition is very much decayed, and the Laboratory is in a most dilapidated state, and presents a cheerless appearance.
>
> The committee propose to cause all the upper appartments of this edifice to be thrown into one large Library room, so that a more convenient arrangement of the books may be made. As it stands, most of the books are entirely out of reach without laborious climbing. But until the exact balance in their hands is ascertained they have not thought it prudent to make this alteration.
>
> The mathematical, Astronomical and chemical apparatus require

considerable repairs, and they recommend that Mr. Alexander Young of Camden be employed to effect them. He is the most competent person within the knowledge of the committee & has expressed to the Chairman his willingness to undertake the repairs. Reports from the Professors of these departments will be necessary to ascertain precisely what is required to be done.

Wm. De Saure, Chairman
Dec 9, 1835

The information contained in this report allows us to trace the changes made during the renovations of 1834–1835. Here, for example, we learn that at this time the massive granite steps which today characterize the entries of the College buildings were erected as replacements for the original wooden steps which had "often been burnt down by the students." LaBorde, who attended the College during the 1820s, has left us a first-hand account of the merriment occasioned by the spectacle of the elderly professors cumbrously entering Rutledge College by ladder:

> The President, Dr. Cooper, was very clumsy, and it was plainly to be seen that he ever regarded it as an enterprise of great hazard, and requiring for its execution great courage . . . he makes the effort, but it is impossible. He has dared, and angels can do no more. He staggers at the first round of the ladder, and plants himself again upon terra firma. But he must enter. He calls for help. He asks Wallace to come down and aid him, but he politely refuses. He renews his effort at ascent, but again fails. He now retires, taking to himself the consolation of a true philosopher, that he had put forth his mightiest strength, and that he had only failed because it was impossible.[18]

The granite steps which ended these gymnastics are stylistically notable, for like the Maxcy Monument, the steps reflect architectural developments far from the College campus. In America, building with large blocks of granite began c. 1805. Such construction was made possible by the discovery of a stone cutting method which facilitated the quarrying of large, rectilinear units of granite. This new technique was first used in Massachusetts and proved to be so popular that by 1824 the newspapers of the day carried references to "the Boston Granite Style." Along the seaboard from Maine to New Orleans buildings composed either wholly or partially of monolithic granite blocks were erected during the second quarter of the nineteenth century. The Charleston Insurance and Trust Co. building (1839) on Broad Street in Charleston exemplifies this phenomenon in South Carolina. The facade of this building is built of large units of granite cut and finished in Quincy, Massachusetts. The design of this facade is based upon Plate 48 of the *Builder's Guide* by Asher Benjamin, a book published in Boston in 1838. And in the South Carolina upcountry, the Boston Granite Style is reflected, albeit crudely, in the form and construction of the steps erected by the Committee on College Repairs.[19]

From the Committee report we also learn that "the whole exterior of both the colleges have been painted and penciled . . . and the buildings now present a fresh and new appearance." This sentence is the most direct evidence we possess as to the early treatment of the brick exterior walls of Rutledge and DeSaussure Colleges. This reference to "painting and penciling" conveys an interesting aspect of early nineteenth-century building practice in Columbia. Due to the shortcomings of local masons and materials, brickwork left much to be desired. One solution to this problem was to paint the entire exterior of the wall surface red, both to give the bricks a more vibrant hue and to obscure the irregularities of the mortar joints. A white lead pigment was then used to delineate a vivid and

[18] Ibid., 132–34.

[19] For a review of the "Boston Granite Style" see John Morrill Bryan, "Boston's Granite Architecture, C. 1810–1860" (unpublished dissertation, Boston University, 1972).

often intricate pattern of false mortar joints upon the wall. Remnants of this technique are visible today under the roof of the rear porch of the Ainsley Hall House in Columbia which was designed by Robert Mills in 1819. Evidence that this was done on a number of the College buildings is found in the construction contracts. Furthermore, the restoration of 1975 uncovered such "penciled" mortar joints on both McCutchen House and DeSaussure College. In explaining this decorative touch we should recall that stone buildings were desired by the Board of Trustees from the beginning; however, as sufficient stone was not available locally, the idea was abandoned and the buildings were built of brick. There was ample precedent for deceptive, superficial treatment of this type. We think here of the Redwood Library in Newport, Rhode Island, designed by Peter Harrison in 1747, or the entry detailing of Thomas Jefferson's Monticello; in both instances wooden elements are beveled and painted with a sand ladened pigment to resemble stone.

William DeSaussure's report of 1835 also helps us to establish the chronology of the construction of the brick wall which once surrounded the South Carolina College. For a long time the need for such a wall had been discussed. On 30 November 1807, for example, the building committee of the Board of Trustees reported to the Board that "your committee conceive the erection of a wall round the College buildings will be one great means of enabling the Faculty to preserve among the Students that good order and decorum so essential to the welfare of the Institution and therefore recommend it as an object of the first importance." The following summer, on 24 June 1808, the Trustees resolved that "The President of the Board be instructed to represent to the Legislature in the name of the Trustees the necessity of surrounding the College with a brick wall and to request that the Board of Trustees be authorized to contract for the building of the said wall." Without waiting for the response of the legislature, the Board voted on 27 June 1808 to pay for "three hundred and thirty lightwood posts used by Mr. Clarke about the College." At the same meeting they "Resolved that the Standing Committee be authorized to have the ground which may be necessary to be enclosed by a wall around the College accurately measured and an estimate of the expence of building a brick wall nine feet high to include the same and that they employ a person to make the said admeasurement and estimate and report the same to the next meeting of the Board." It would appear that the Board authorized the erection of a wooden fence, perhaps the one that appears in the Ulor painting, in 1808. But for quite some time nothing more was done about constructing a permanent brick wall. More than a decade passed, and Jonathan Maxcy wrote, in one of his last letters to the Board:

> Gentlemen,
>
> I beg leave to submit to your consideration the following things, which in my opinion, are essential to the prosperity of the South Carolina College: viz—
>
> 1. The establishment of a more comprehensive system of laws, for the government and instruction of the college.
>
> 2. The appointment of professors who shall be constantly resident in the College, and who shall constantly board in Commons with the students.
>
> . . . .
>
> 4. The building of a suitable fence or wall round the College Edifices. —The necessity of accomplishing these things, is so apparent, that I forbear to add any remarks. . . .
>
> Jonathan Maxcy[20]

[20] A letter from Jonathan Maxcy to the Board of Trustees, transmitted to the legislature on 6 December 1820 by John Geddes, President of the Board. SCAH.

That a substantial wall was "essential to the prosperity of the college" was self-evident to President Maxcy. He must have winced remembering the petition of Malachi Howell, a Columbian whose home abutted the campus. In 1816 Howell claimed that the location of the College made the area unfit for residential development and he requested, unsuccessfully, that the state compensate him for the adverse effect upon the value of his property.[21] Recognizing that good fences make good neighbors, the Trustees had attempted on several occasions to acquire the money to build a wall during the presidency of Dr. Maxcy. No such efforts were made while Thomas Cooper served as President of the College. William DeSaussure's report of 9 December 1835, tells us that the Committee on College Repairs, prompted by "the air of dilapidation and decay which the ragged wooden fences about the colleges always presented," made contracts for the construction of a permanent brick wall. DeSaussure's next significant report makes it clear that the new brick wall was virtually completed within a year. On 2 December 1836, he wrote that

> The Committee on College repairs submit the following account of the fund of $20,000 appropriated by the Legislature for that purpose, and of the work done & unpaid for and of that which remains to be done.
>
> By the account submitted it will be seen that the Committee have expended the sum of $19870.50 and that there remains in their hands the sum of $129.50.
>
> | For repairs & the wall there yet remain [*illegible*] | |
> |---|---|
> | to Thomas Dain bricklayer | 998.05 |
> | to John G. Brown for bricks | 1510.95 |
> | to Thomas H Wade carpenter | 37.25 |
> | | $2546.25 |
>
> Leaving the sum of two thousand five hundred and forty six dollars and twenty five cents yet unpaid, for work done & materials purchased from which deduct the amount in hand of $129.50 and there remains the sum of $2416.75 to be provided for. This excess beyond the amount appropriated the committee could not anticipate nor prevent. The repairs were of such a character that no specific costs could be made in relation to them, and no estimate procured. The committee contracted upon very reasonable terms for a supply of bricks adequate according to the estimate furnished by the bricklayer to complete the wall & all the other work about the college—but that estimate fell far short of the amount actually required, and when it became necessary to contract for the quantity necessary to complete the work, the price of bricks had risen very considerably, and has been rising ever since.
>
> In relation to lime of which a great quantity was required, the committee contracted for a supply in Charleston which according to the estimates furnished them was sufficient to complete the work; but such was the very inferior character of all the lime brought to this market during the last season that instead of a barrel of lime producing two barrels and a quarter when slacked, it hardly exceeded its original bulk. Before the repairs and the wall had reached their present state the committee were made aware that the sum appropriated would not be adequate to meet the expence, but upon consultation they resolved to assume the responsibility of completing the work, being persuaded that the Board would sanction their proceeding.
>
> The work *not yet* done, but which is of an indispensable nature will require the following sums
>
> | | |
> |---|---|
> | Bricks to finish the wall | $256.25 |
> | Bricklayer for laying | 75. |
> | Iron gate & crop fences & trim the wall | 45. |
> | | 376.25 |
> | | 2416.75 |
> | | $2793.00 |

[21] Report of the Committee on Claims, John S. Cogdell, Chairman, 11 December 1816. SCAH.

Your committee recommend that application be made to the Legislature for appropriation of the above sum of two thousand seven hundred and ninety three dollars for the purpose of meeting the above deficit.

W. F. DeSaussure, Chairman

This apologetic memorandum, recounting the tribulations of the Committee on College Repairs, documents the fact that work on the brick wall surrounding the campus was virtually completed by December 1836. But in 1836 the Trustees were not content merely to enhance the existing facilities, and as their various maintenance and improvement projects neared completion, they began to explore the need for wholly new buildings. Thus, on 8 December 1836, Mr. McCord as Chairman of the

Committee on additional accommodations for students etc. submitted a report as follows—

The committee to whom was referred the resolution that a committee of three be appointed to inquire and report what additional accommodations will be required for the lodging of the students and the amount of appropriations which will be required for any additional buildings which may be necessary for that purpose, and for repairs and alterations to the present buildings beg leave to report

That they have not yet had time to make temporary arrangements for the accommodation of students, but are satisfied that two new buildings are necessary for these accommodations, and think it most convenient and compatible with the present arrangement, that one building should be placed between the present Library, and the new Professor's House, and another of the same size on the opposite side near to the Stewards House. These two apartments to be large enough to accommodate fifty students, each having a sleeping room with a common sitting room for every two.

The committee are entirely of the opinion that the present building used for that purpose as a Library is unfit for that purpose. Besides, the imminent danger which must be daily incurred in having the chemical laboratory, the Library and mechanical and Philosophical apparatus in the same House. The present building is entirely out of repair, the sleepers and partitions in the lower part of the house being entirely decayed and ready to fall, the roof leaks and the floors are rotten. The committee recommend that a new building, entirely separate from the other buildings be erected for the use of the Library.

In this report we find "the new Professor's House," Lieber College (Figure 35), mentioned along with the initial proposal for the construction of Elliot (Figure 36) and Pinckney (Figure 37) Colleges and the South Caroliniana Library (Figure 38). Not much is known about the source of the design of Lieber College. An appropriation of $10,000 for its construction was authorized by the legislature in 1835; the building contract was signed by Thomas H. Wade on 5 May 1836; and on 13 December 1837 W. F. DeSaussure reported to the Committee on Public Buildings that the structure was complete. In both plan and elevation Lieber College appears to be a segment of a Philadelphia row-house rather than a detached dwelling. On the college campus it is an interesting aberration; it is unfortunate that we cannot explain its origins. Be that as it may, it is significant that the report recommends the extension of the balanced horseshoe ground plan in the siting of the two dormitories and presupposes the replication of the interior plans employed in Rutledge and DeSaussure. The need for the recommended dormitories was self-evident, as some 150 students were then enrolled although the College buildings could only accommodate 100. The Board of Trustees quickly acted upon the McCord report. On 10 December 1836 George McDuffie, as President of the Board, wrote to Senator James R. Gregg:

FIGURE 35. Lieber College, from a photograph by Judith Steinhauser.

Columbia, 10th Dec. 1836

Sir:

The Board of Trustees have directed me to communicate to the Legislature, a resolution recently adopted, requesting an appropriation of sixty thousand dollars for the following purposes viz

For erecting a building for the accommodation of the students	$25,000
for a Library Hall	15,000
for books	5,000
for general repairs	10,000

I have deemed it most expedient to communicate this information to the Chairman of the proper Committee in each house, and to request that they will bring it before their respective Houses in the mode deemed most proper.

Your obt sert

Geo. McDuffie[22]

These few lines effectively portray the ambitions of the Board during the Barnwell administration. Here they requested the largest appropriation for buildings in the history of the College: They proposed to virtually double the space available to students. The aspirations of the Board were matched by the generosity of the legislature and the appropriation was granted without delay. A committee of the Trustees was established to direct the disbursement of these funds, and the first report of this committee, on 2 December 1837, gives us the chronology of the dormitory project:

> The committee appointed by your honorable body in Dec last to superintend the erection of new college buildings, and to apply to the several specific objects the sums designated in the appropriation of $60,000, granted to the college by the Legislature beg leave respectfully to report

[22] MS. "Communication of the President of the Board of Trustees of the South Ca. College in relation to an appropriation for College buildings." SCAH.

That your committee early in January last advertized in the principal cities from Boston to Charleston inviting contractors to make proposals for erecting two college wings, giving all the necessary information as to price of materials, mechanics labor etc. The 15th March was fixed on as the time for giving out the contract, when several bids were received the procedings continued—Philadelphia, Baltimore, Virginia & from persons in this place, varying in amount from $26,000 to $45,000—Believing that the building could not be erected for a sum less than the lowest bid, from all the information your committee could gain, a contract was made with Messers Wade & Davis. who entered into bond for the faithful execution of the work. To be completed within a specified time viz. one of the wings, on or before the first of Dec next & the other on or before 1st March 1838. One building is already finished & now occupied by students & the other will be completed by 1 Jan next.

The contract "with Messers Wade & Davis" has survived; its specifications contain a great deal of information about these buildings.

South Carolina
Richland District

Articles of agreement between Thos. H. Wade and Thos Davis of the one part, and R. W. Barnwell, W. F. Desaussure, D. J. McCord, Jas. Gregg, & Thomas [*illegible*], Commissioners, appointed by the Board of Trustees of the South Carolina College.

That the said Thos. H. Wade, & Thos. Davis agree to construct & build two college wings in the campus, for the accomodation of students of the S. C. College. Each wing to be ninety by thirty feet out & out, & three stories high—The first story eleven feet in the clear; the second story ten feet in the clear—the third story nine feet in the clear—To be built of brick laid in good lime mortar, in the proportion of one barrel of good stone lime to every twelve hundred brick, & in the proportion of one bushel of new slacked lime to three bushels of sharp sand—The foundation to be two and one half feet deep four bricks or thirty six inches at bottom, [*illegible*] after the ground has been thoroughly compressed. The first six courses to drop off successively from thirty six to twenty two inches, & run up that thickness to the first floor—The walls of the first & second stories to be eighteen inches thick—the third story fourteen inches thick—The centre partition walls to be eighteen inches thick as the foundation, & thence upwards fourteen inches thick in the first & second stories, & nine inches thick in the third story, between the chimney & outer walls there is to be a brick cornice; & a parapet wall all round to hide the roof nine inches in thickness, with square recesses in the spaces immediately over the windows—rough cast. The first floor to be one foot above the ground on the highest point of the site, or four and a half feet from the foundation.

First Story

The first story of each wing is to have 16 windows of 18 lights each, 10 by 12 [*illegible*] [doors] six panel, worked on both sides, 1¾ inch thick—four entry doors, six panels, worked on both sides—usual size—eight batten doors for dormitories—four doors for closets, & four stout mantel pieces—the closets to be finished with shelves—& each dormitory to have a strip with pins for clothes. The door frames from the entry to each room, & the window frames to be finished with suitable architrave & bak moulding. The jams to closet & dormitory doors to be finished with moulded edges.

The floor joists 3 x 10 inches, laid 17 inches from center to center [*illegible*] to have their bearing on the wall. Flooring plank to be tongue and groove stuff [*illegible*] inches wide, tongued, grooved, & secret nails. Wainscot around all of the rooms 2½ feet high with a [*illegible*] surbase—all clean, well seasoned stuff. All of the walls, & ceiling to be lathed & plastered, [*illegible*] a small window over each outer door, 8 lights, 10 by 12. All of the doors to have 7 inch, 3 bolt, brass knob licks Doors to be hung with 4 inch, butts. Solid window frames sash 1¾ inch thick. The stairs to be finished with rail & counter rail, & risers mitred to string.

FIGURE 36. Elliott College, from a photograph by Judith Steinhauser.

FIGURE 37 *right.* Pinckney College, from a photograph by Judith Steinhauser.

Third Story
Second Story

In every respect the third story is to [*destroyed*]

The roof to have a rise of not less than 3 feet, & to be covered with tin. The whole of the interior wood work to be painted with 3 coats, all white, except the mantel pieces, washer boards, & stair cases. The first two are to be black, & the latter slate or chocolate color. The exterior is to be painted red, in oil colours, & penciled with white lead. There are to be three [*destroyed*] The steps & door dells to be granite, window sills & caps, on the front of each building, also door caps, are to be freestone.

Tin gutters, & conductors at the two corners of the west end of each Building to convey water from the roof & from the foundation, The whole of the work is to be done in a neat, substantial, & workmanlike manner, & the contractors are to furnish all of the materials of every kind. The materials to be of the very best quality that can be procured, & work to be done according to the plan signed at the same time with this contract until the said buildings are finished, & received by the commissioners, the said contractors agree to be responsible for the same—and the said contractors agree that one of the said buildings shall be finished & delivered on or before the 1st day of Dec next, and the other on or before the 1st day of March next, & that in the event of their failure they will forfeit twenty per cent upon the whole amount thereof. And the said R. W. Barnwell, W. F. Desaussure, D. F. McCord, Jas. Gregg, & Thomas [*illegible*] commissioners as aforesaid, agree to with the said Thos. H. Wade, & Thos. Davis to pay them the sum of Twenty six thousand dollars, in the following manner, viz: six thousand dollars on signing this contract, with bond & security. One half of the remainder when the said two buildings shall be ready to be covered [*illegible*] the balance on the completion & delivery of said buildings.

In consideration whereof we have hereto set our hands & seals this third day of March in the year [*destroyed*]

R. W. Barnwell — Tho H. Wade
Thomas [*illegible*] — Thos Davis

FIGURE 38. The South Caroliniana Library, from a photograph by Judith Steinhauser.

Here we find the number and size of window panes in the original sash, the configuration of door panels, elements of the interior color scheme and hardware, and the treatment of the brick exterior which was to be "painted red, in oil colours, & penciled with white lead." This phrase tells us that the exterior walls of these buildings were painted red to give the brick a more vibrant hue; false mortar joints were then "penciled" onto the wall surface to disguise the irregularities of the masonry. The surviving documents suggest that the dormitories were constructed without complications and were completed on schedule. On 9 May 1838 President Barnwell reported to the Trustees that "Our new college buildings have been finished and are now occupied. The plan has been agreed upon for our new library, but no contract has yet been made for the execution of the work."

The efforts of President Barnwell to refurbish the facilities of the College culminated in the construction of the South Caroliniana Library. Discussion concerning a new library began in the fall of 1836; the completion of plans for the building was announced on 8 May 1838; and on 6 May 1840 President Barnwell announced to the Board of Trustees that the library was finished. The chronology of the South Caroliniana project is historically notable for it appears to have been the first separate library facility operated by a college or university in the United States. Harvard, it is interesting to note, did not have a building devoted exclusively to its libraries until 1841. The first Yale library building was begun in 1843 and finished in 1846. Princeton did not have a separate library until 1873.

In reviewing the development of the South Caroliniana Library we must bear in mind several of the factors which prompted the construction. There was, by 1836, an acceptance of the importance of the College to the well-being of the state; concurrently, library facilities were considered central to the work of the College. Thus, despite the fact that annual appropriations for the purchase of library materials did not begin until 1838, significant funds were allocated sporadically for that purpose. The requests for library funds evoke the ardent support that the library enjoyed. The enthusiastic grandiloquence of these requests conjures up visions of the collections of the South Carolina College Library—row upon stately row of leather-bound incunabula, of gilt lettering upon a crimson field. Alfred Huger, for example, in requesting such an appropriation in 1825, spoke to his colleagues in the legislature saying:

> The Committee on the College to whom was refer'd so much of the Governor's message as related to the South Carolina College beg leave to report that they have attentively considered the same, and recommend that Five ($5000) thousand dollars be appropriated for the purchase of Books for the college library. Your committee in suggesting to your honorable body the expediency of making this appropriation are influenced by those considerations which they believe are strongly impressed upon the minds of their fellow citizens at large. They are directed by those views which a succession of enlightened Legislatures have invariably taken of the invaluable institution. They are prone to indulge in those feelings which they believe are prominent in the Bosom of Every Lover of Letters and Every Lover of his Country. They believe that the best system of economy which can be adopted is to protect and encourage the dissemination of all useful knowledge. In contemplating the advantages which are daily accruing to the state from the establishment of this institution your committee cannot refrain from repeating what they have often expressed, their unbounded respect for the wisdom and patriotism of those men whose names are recorded as the founders of this monument of their intelligence and virtue. Tis the policy of tyrants to entrammell the human understanding & the privilege of despotism to darken the intellect of slaves. Tis the security of Freedom that *her* sons are enlightened, and the boast of Republicans that theirs is the doctrine of Equal Rights, which can alone be maintained by the diffusion of general & correct information. Tis for them to remember that Knowl-

edge is Power and their Liberty is safe, but should they ever forget that political strength is but another name for learning and for Science, and that Liberty is endangered. Your committee feel no disposition to dwell upon a subject which is already so well understood or unnecessarily to urge a continuance of your patronage, when they believe that its influence is so universally acknowledged. In every corner of your state and in every department of your government the living evidences that your liberality has been rewarded are preeminently conspicuous. The Flowers of Literature are blooming in every valley, and the tree which puts forth good fruit is dispensing its blessings from the tops of your mountains to the shores of the Atlantic. Tis for you to admire this beautifull picture, to cultivate this garden which has been seeded by yourselves and to leave to your posterity the abundant harvest which its fertility will ensure them.[23]

The success of this appeal indicates that the sentiments of Alfred Huger were widely shared. As a direct result of this support, the expanding collections of reading materials, and the increasing use of these by a growing student body, placed an ever-increasing burden upon the facilities which housed the library. Initially the collections were located in the room above the chapel in Rutledge College. Outgrowing this space, the library was moved in 1815 to the upper floor of the new Library and Science Building. Here it remained for twenty-three years. But in its new location it was unfortunately subject to the "noxious fumes" of the laboratory below and "prey to the perpetual danger of fire" from the chemicals stored amongst the scientific apparatus. As if this were not enough, the limited space forced the use of extremely high shelving so that "laborious climbing was necessary to reach most of the books."[24] In short, conditions were such that when the Committee on College Repairs found the Library and Science Building to be in a state of dilapidation, they immediately recommended that an entirely new and separate building be constructed for the library. Thus on 8 December 1836, the committee reported to the Board that "the present building used for the Library is unfit for that purpose—the lower part of the house being entirely decayed and ready to fall; the roof leaks and the floors are rotten. The committee recommend that a new building entirely separate from the other buildings be erected for the use of the Library." Two days later the Trustees requested the money to erect a "Library Hall."

Columbia, 10th Decr 1836

Sir:

The Board of Trustees have directed me to communicate to the Legislature, a resolution recently adopted, requesting an appropriation of sixty thousand dollars for the following purposes. viz.

For erecting a building for the accommodation of the students	$25,000
For a Library Hall	15,000
For Books	5,000
For repairing Stewards house	5,000
For general repairs.	10,000
	$60,000

I have deemed it most expedient to communicate this information to the Chairman of the proper Committee in each House, and to request that they will bring it before their respective Houses in the manner deemed most proper.

Your Obt sert
Geo. McDuffie[25]

[23] MS. "Report of the Committee on the College, In the Senate 15 Dec. 1825." SCAH.

[24] Green, "Library," *Bulletin of the University of South Carolina*, VII (October, 1906), 2.

[25] Note 23 above.

The conceptual development of the South Caroliniana Library poses a conundrum. We know the chronology of the project. We have the building contracts and specifications. The sources of the design itself are demonstrable, and yet the name of a specific designer eludes us. One historian has stated that "the plans were prepared by the professors."[26] This assertion, however, is not substantiated by extant documents. It is true that a formally appointed Library Committee existed in 1839 (A. B. Longstreet, W. F. DeSaussure, J. P. Carroll, and J. H. Thornwell), but the relationship of this committee to the drafting of the plans is nowhere specified. Given the complexity of the library in both plan and decorative detail, it seems most unlikely that the sole surviving reference to the development of the library connotes creativity by the Committee. On 9 May 1838, President Barnwell told the Trustees that "the plan has been agreed upon for our new library but no contract has yet been made for the execution of the work." This brief statement is all we have concerning the origins of the plan, but references in the building's contract to seven architectural drawings, now lost, suggest the involvement of a person or persons with technical training. The contract is quoted here in its entirety:

> Know all men by these presents that we, Charles Beck and James Boatwright are held and firmly bound unto the Trustees of the South Carolina College in the sum of twenty-thousand dollars, to be paid by said Trustees, their successors & assigns, to which payment we bind ourselves and each and every one [*illegible*] executors and administrators, jointly and severally firmly by these presents sealed with our seals and dated this tenth day of October the year of our lord one thousand eight hundred and thirty eight.
>
> The condition of this obligation is such that if the said Charles Beck shall well truely and faithfully perform this contract with said Trustees contained on this sheet of paper and the one pencilled annexed, bearing cover date with these presents, then this obligation to be void and of none effect or else to remain in full force and virtue.
>
> Signed, sealed & delivered in presence of
> C. M. Beck
> James Boatwright
>
> This indenture made and entered into by and between Charles Beck of the one part and the Trustees of the South Carolina College of the other part.
>
> Witnesseth, that the said Charles Beck has agreed and hereby does agree to build for the South Carolina College on such site within the college grounds, as may be designated by the building committee of the said trustees, a college library and deliver the said completely finished in the very best workmanlike manner, on or before the first day of October next, according to the plans and specifications hereunto annexed, for the sum of twenty thousand dollars. Three thousand dollars thereof to be paid him on signing this contract, and the balance in such sums as the work progresses, that not more than three fourths of the work done shall be paid for at any time before the entire building is finished and received, in which payment the said Charles shall receive from J. G. Brown all the bricks necessary for the said building, at the price of twelve dollars the thousand, delivered at the site of the building, to be included in the [*illegible*] payment.
>
> Plans and Specifications
>
> The plans of the building contained in the seven drawings accompanying this contract marked Nos 1. 2. 3. 4. 5. 6. & 7. and endorsed by the said Charles and the chairman of the said building committee, are in every respect to constitute a part of this contract, and the library is to be built of the best materials and finished in the very best stile of architecture according thereto, except when in these specifications deviations therefrom are stipulated for.
>
> Nos. 1 & 2 represent the basement story and the front elevation of the building. The columns of the portico are to be of brick rough cast, with granite plints and free stone capitals, and the cornice

[26] Green, *History of the University*, 276.

above to be of wood, the whole to be painted in immitation of granite or freestone as the committee may direct. The belting course above the basement story in front and all the window sills are to be of freestone, the sills of the front and back doors in the basement are to be of granite. The rest of the building is to be of brick laid in the best morter, made of stone lime and clean worked sand, filling the entire wall. The walls of the foundation are to be on a foundation dug two feet deep and well rammed, and twenty seven inches thick; the basement story walls are to be eighteen inches thick and above they are to be fourteen inches thick, except in front, on each side of the recesses of the windows, they are to be eighteen inches thick. The platform under the portico is to be twelve feet wide and curbed with granite, and paved with brick. The passage in the basement story is to be entirely finished, but the two rooms, on each side of it, are to be left unfinished, except that all the doors are to be completed; the shutters made painted and hung with proper fastenings, and two flues are to be carried up in each room.

No 3 represents the floor and plan of the library in the second story. In this room the two doors on each side of the fire places are to be mere imitations, and two of the stair cases into the galleries are to be omitted, and in place of these, two closets are to be substituted, properly finished within. On the back of the building there are to be two windows in this story to correspond in all respects with those in front and two blanks are to be formed externally in place of windows.

No 4 represents the alcoves and galleries, which are to be finished precisely in the same manner as the congressional library at Washington of which [*illegible*] is a drawing. The whole is to be finished in the best stile and all the recesses and galleries to be shelved ready to receive the library. The distances between the shelves are to be settled by the committee.

No 5 represents the finish of the two ends of the library, in which there is to be no change except that the mantle pieces are to be of wood moulded and painted in imitation of marble.

No 6 represents the ceiling overhead, which is to be done in plaster in the very best stile, equal to that of the congressional library, with the exception that instead of its being coved, it is to be straight.

No 7 represents the back projection of the building & stair case. This projection is to be carried up as high as the parrapet, to be finished with stucco cornisse within, and covered with a tin roof.

The roof of the building is to be covered with tin with such declivities from the centre as will make it perfect free from leaks and the water is to be carried off, in gutters and [*illegible*] tin pipes extending to the ground of proper size and with proper fastenings & heads. The seven windows in the library are to be furnished with inside shutters formed to fold into the jams of the wall on each side & the circular heads of those windows are to be filled with stationary venetian blinds—the glazing of these windows shall be with the best Boston crown glass. The lower sashes to be hung with weights. The whole interior of the library shall be painted dead white except the shelvings, which shall be painted on the edges with green and excepting the doors, which shall be painted in imitation of oak. The stair case is to have a heavy hand railing of mahogany.

Where any of these specifications or plans are imperfect as to the manner in which the work is to be done the work shall be done in a stile corresponding with the design of the rest of the building. Witness our hands this tenth day of October 1838

sealed & delivered C. Beck
in the presence of R. Barnwell
W. F. DeSaussure building committee
G. Gregg
Blanding[27]

This contract contains a great deal of useful information. The central point, of course, is that Charles M. Beck agreed to build the library for $20,000. Through the financial records of the College his name is associated with the Caroliniana project from start to finish, but beyond this, we know nothing about him. His relative obscurity, particularly the fact that he is not known to have designed any

[27] The library contracts and specifications are to be found in the Miscellaneous Files of the SCL.

prominent buildings, would seem to suggest that he did not compose the seven drawings referred to in the contract "Plans and Specifications." The loss of these drawings is galling, for the descriptions of them presented in the contract suggest an intricate and sophisticated rendering. It is clear that these drawings contained a number of details which would have been beyond the ken of a local contractor or the College Building Committee. The use of the Congressional Library as a model for the piano noble, the library room on the elevated principal floor, was ambitious. The Congressional Library in the Capitol in Washington, D.C., was quite ornate, its alcoves were framed by composite pilasters and its coved ceiling was articulated by complex panels. Other notable stipulations contained in the Caroliniana contract include the projecting stairwell, the use of four false doors to give the appearance of symmetry in the library room, the detailing of the shutters, and the extensive use of deception in the finishing of the details—the mantle pieces were "to be of wood . . . painted in immitation of granite or freestone," and the doors were to be painted "in immitation of oak."

In discussing the Caroliniana a number of writers have stated that it was designed by Robert Mills. Heretofore this assertion has never been substantiated by documents of any type.[28] This attribution has been adduced from the fact that Robert Mills left Columbia in 1830 and went to Washington; there, in 1836, he accepted the position of Federal Architect. From this vantage point he was ideally situated to send recommendations and drawings of the Library of Congress to the Building Committee of the South Carolina College. Fortunately, we no longer need to rely upon such tenuous circumstantial evidence. The discovery of a set of drawings in an unpublished Robert Mills diary demonstrates his participation in the development of the South Caroliniana Library.[29] These schematic drawings (Figures 39, 40, 41, and 42) and the accompanying notations present the intended site plan, six elevations, six ground plans, preliminary measurements and cost estimates. It should first be noted that these sketches are indubitably schemata for the College library, for the captions, written in Mills' hand, include "Library and Hall of the College S C.," "West Facade of Library & Hall," "wrote Mr. Ridgeway, Columbia, Sept 19th for extension of time for Design." Moreover, across the entablature of one of the elevations we find "Library" writ large, and "Library & Hall" designates the intended use of the rotunda in one of the ground plans. Finally, the drawings are dated "Jany 27th 1837," that is, at the outset of the library project.

These drawings depict a structure far more elaborate than anything ever built by the College; nevertheless, it is here that we find the seeds of the library plan finally adopted by the Board. The plan of the first story with its central carriage-way flanked by subsidiary storage rooms is analogous to the entry level as constructed; indeed, the carriage passage the Mills proposed through the building explains the ungainly proportions of the present entry hall. The "Principal Floor" of Mills' design consists of a domed rotunda, utilized as a reading room, with storage space in the wings at either end of the building. Here Mills is basically making a utilitarian modification of Thomas Jefferson's design of the library at the

[28] Hollis, *South Carolina College*, 135. Hollis presents the nub of this "old campus legend" on page 296, note 64, when he says, "The tradition that Mills designed the Library has had wide circulation. See, for example, the *Dictionary of American Biography*, XIII, 12: also *The Art Bulletin*, XXIII (September, 1941), 221–22. If Mills, who by this time had acquired an extensive reputation as an architect, had any part in planning the building his name would probably have been mentioned in the official records. An architect (unnamed) was sent to Washington to copy the design of Charles Bulfinch's Library of Congress Room. Margaret Babcock Meriwether in *The State*, October 5, 1941."

[29] Robert Mills, manuscript diary in the Library of Congress.

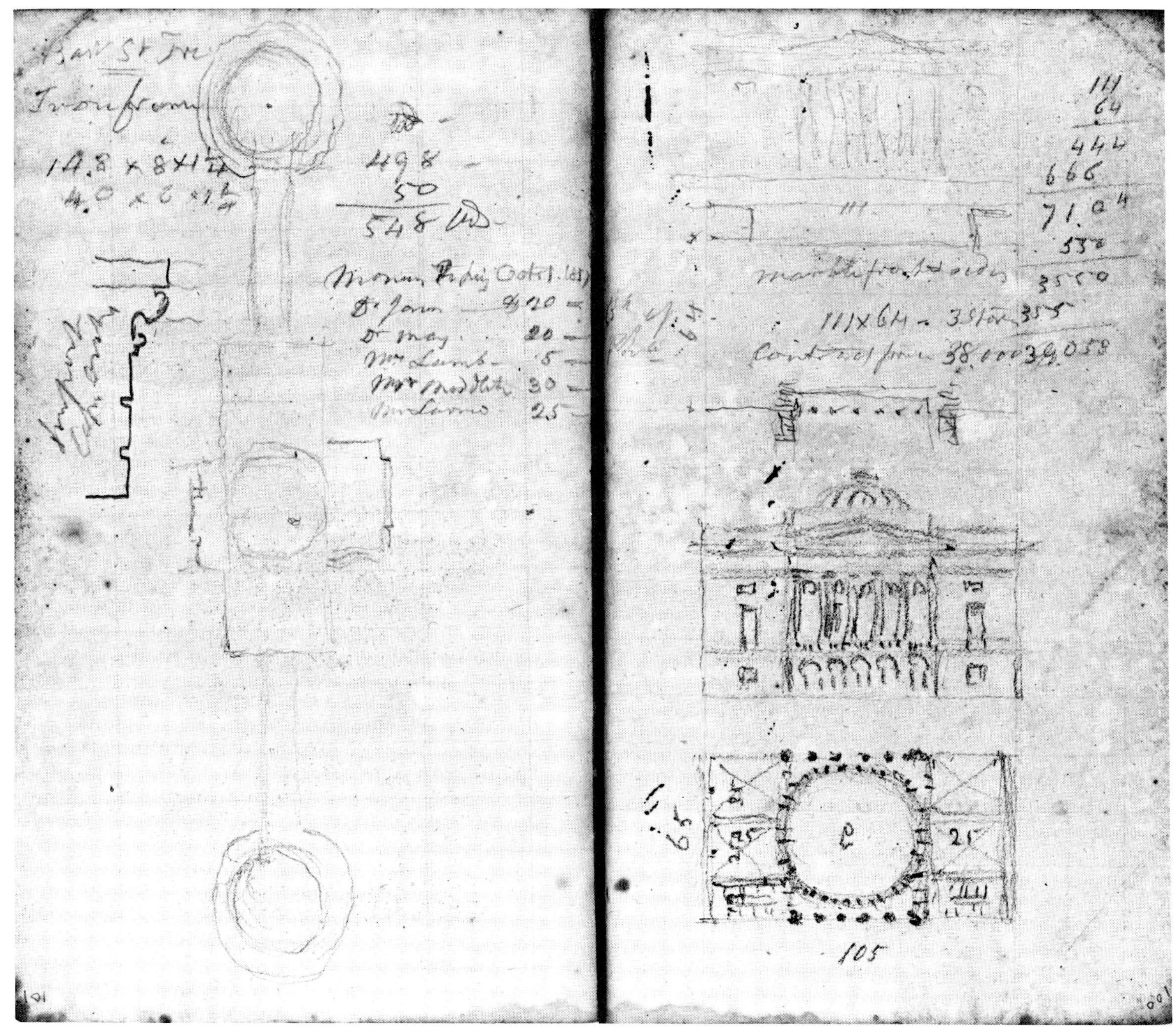

FIGURE 39. Sketches for the South Caroliniana Library, 1837, from the diary of Robert Mills in the collection of the Library of Congress.

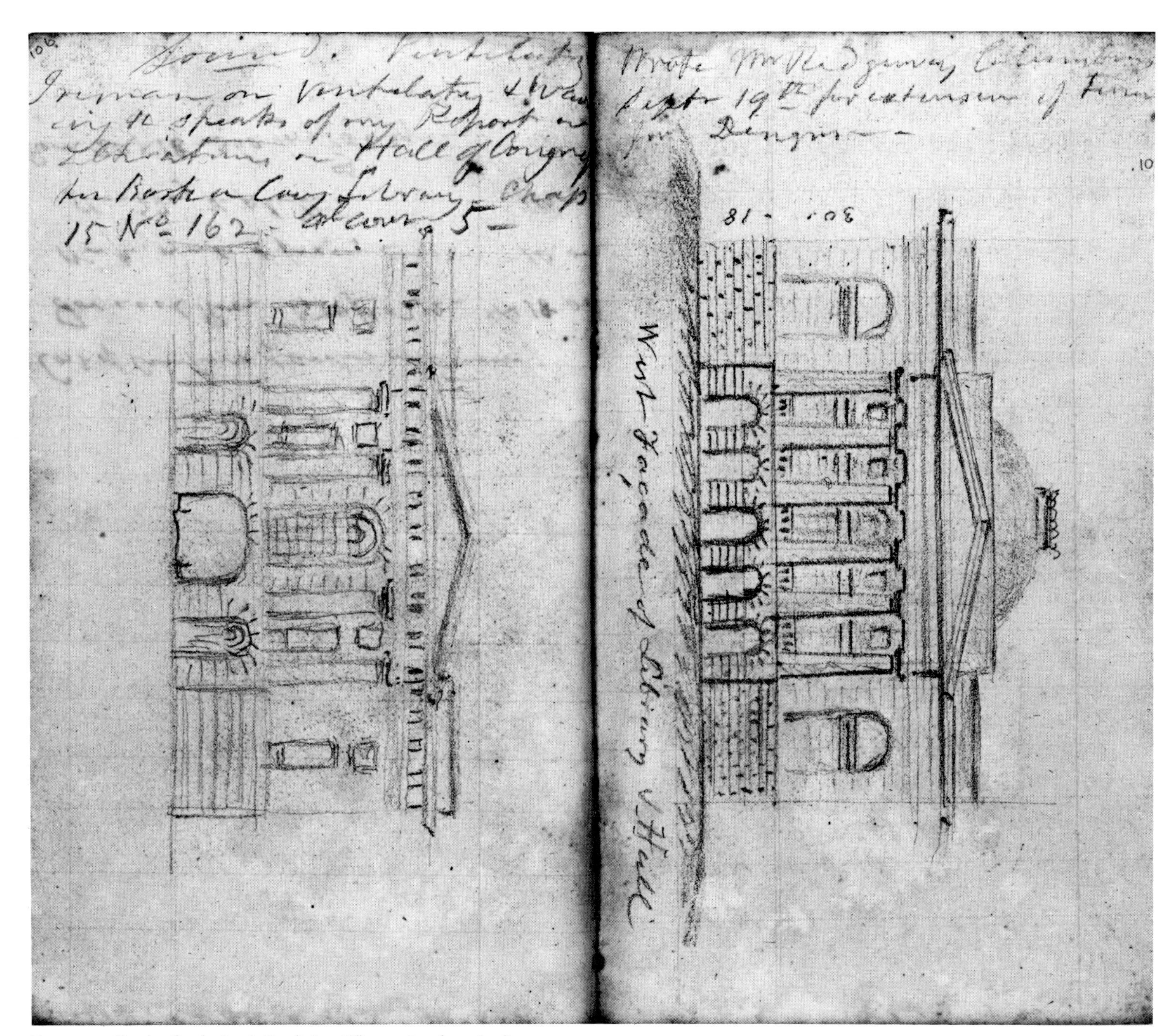

FIGURE 40. Sketches for the South Caroliniana Library, 1837, from the diary of Robert Mills in the collection of the Library of Congress.

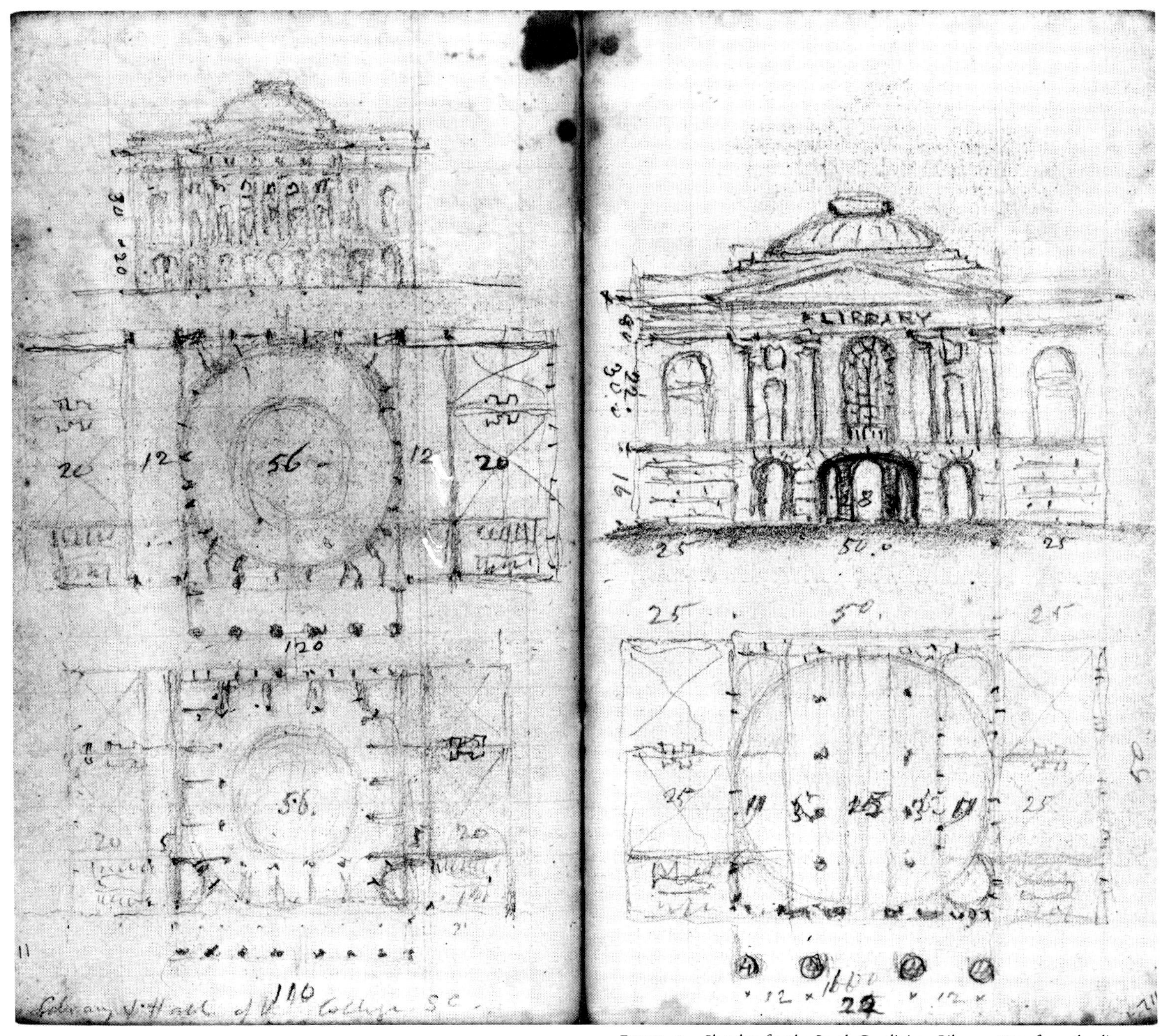

FIGURE 41. Sketches for the South Caroliniana Library, 1837, from the diary of Robert Mills in the collection of the Library of Congress.

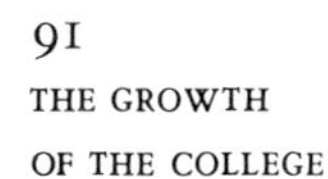

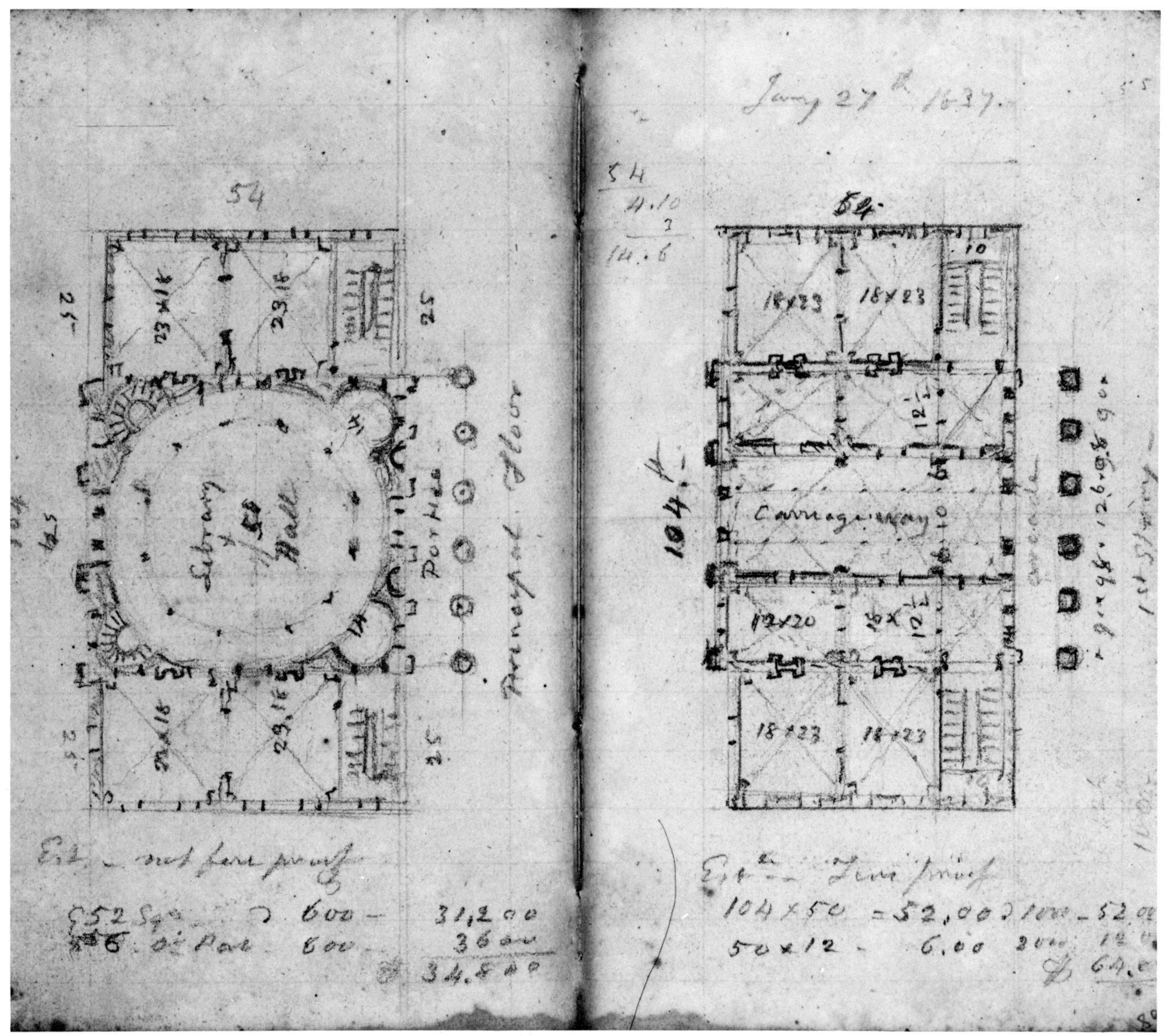

FIGURE 42. Sketches for the South Caroliniana Library, 1837, from the diary of Robert Mills in the collection of the Library of Congress.

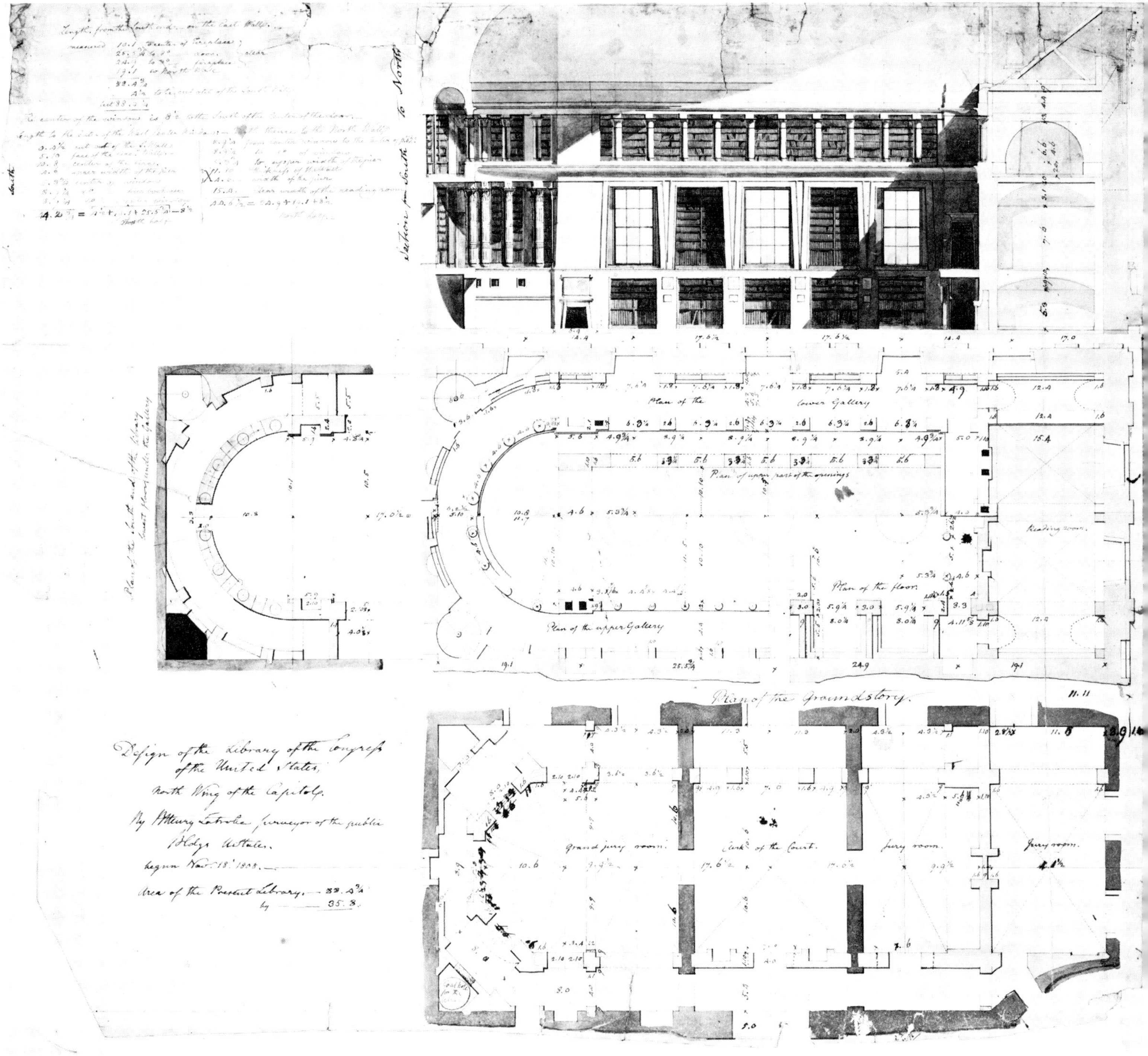

Section from South to North

Plan of the lower Gallery

Plan of upper part of the openings

Reading room

Plan of the floor

Plan of the upper Gallery

Plan of the South end of the Library lowest floor under the Gallery

Plan of the Groundstory.

Grand jury room. Clerk of the Court. Jury room. Jury room.

Design of the Library of the Congress
of the United States,
North Wing of the Capitol.
By B Henry Latrobe, Surveyor of the public
Bldgs U States.
begun Nov. 18. 1808.
Area of the Present Library, 88.4¾
by 35.8.

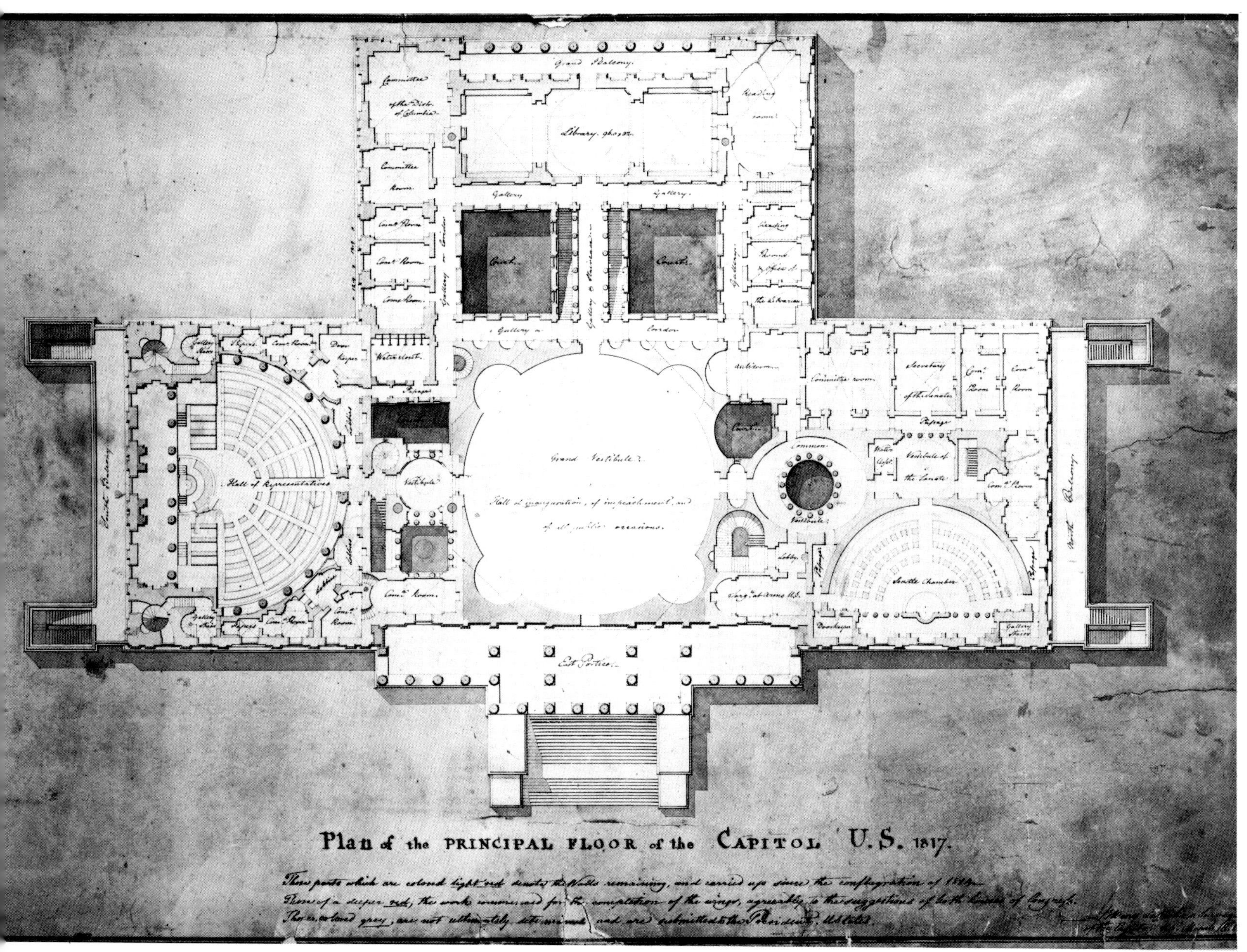

FIGURE 43 *left.* "Design of the Library of the Congress of the United States, North Wing of the Capitol, by B. Henry Latrobe, Nov. 18, 1808," from the collection of the Library of Congress.

FIGURE 44 *above.* "Plan of the principal floor of the Capitol, U.S. 1817, B. Henry Latrobe," from the collection of the Library of Congress.

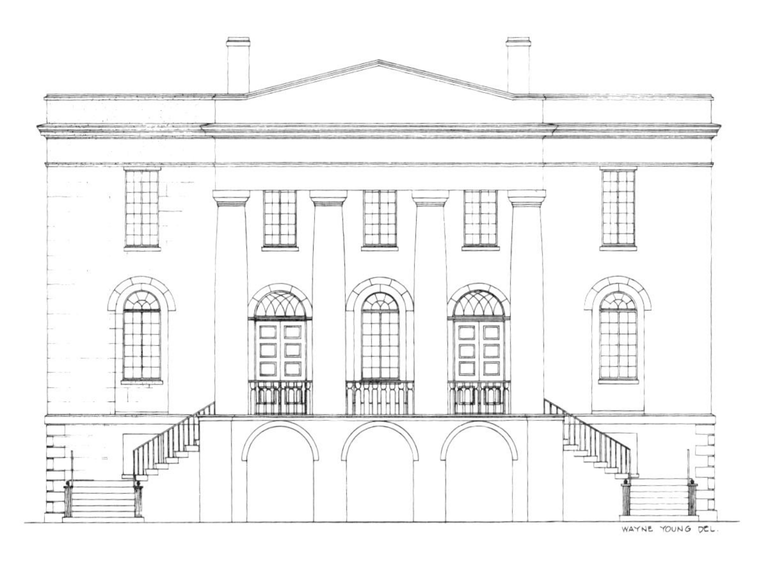

FIGURE 45. A Comparison of the Fireproof Building, Charleston, South Carolina, 1822, by Robert Mills, and the South Caroliniana Library: drawings by Wayne Young.

University of Virginia, and this disposition of space—a reading room flanked by stack space—is mirrored in the executed project.

As only $15,000 had been budgeted for the building, the Trustees must have gasped at Mills' projected costs of $38,800 "Est—not fire proof" and $64,000 "Est—Fire proof." We can imagine them deciding that they could make do without the dome, determining instead to substitute a rectilinear "Library & Hall" in place of the proposed rotunda. Here, as previous historians have suggested, they must have turned to the precedent found in the Library of Congress. Perhaps they did confer with Robert Mills on this point, for we find in drawings of the Library of Congress, signed "BHenry Latrobe" and dated 1808 the prototype of the South Caroliniana Library (Figures 43 and 44). These drawings were executed while Robert Mills was working in Latrobe's office, and upon examining them closely we see a rectangular room with a central entry, five windows, and book storage provided in alcoves and along a balcony; in the ceiling plan we note the three skylights. Excepting the coved ceiling, the reading room of the South Caroliniana Library could almost be reconstructed from these particular drawings.

We can now point to these plans and to Mills' access to them as strong presumptive evidence that he participated in the modification of the designs that appear in his diary. Before concluding our consideration of Mills'sketches, we should note that he labeled the principal elevation as the "West Facade of Library & Hall." This can only mean that he intended the building to face onto Sumter Street, to use the library carriage-way as the gateway to the College grounds. This would have transformed the horseshoe into a quadrangle; it would have also created a visual axis through the archway, past the Maxcy Monument, to the President's House.

Beyond such documentation of Mills' participation in the initial conception and the subsequent modifications of the plan, we should note that during the restoration of the library in 1974–1975, the architect John Califf, Jr., observed that the facade of the Caroliniana is directly derived from the facade of the Fireproof Building (Figure 45) in Charleston which was designed by Robert Mills and built between 1822 and 1827. A comparative drawing of these facades demonstrates that the library is a mirror image of the earlier building, minus its basement story. The congruity is too close to be coincidental.

Yet another aspect of the Caroliniana that is related specifically to the work of Robert Mills is the treatment of the principal stairway. As we enter the library we come into a low, wide hallway which terminates in the stairs leading to the library room. This stairway curves upward and turns an arc of 180° before it reaches the principal floor. The curve of the stair is housed in a semicircular bay which projects from the center of the rear facade of the building. Such a protuberance was unusual in the architecture of South Carolina, but Robert Mills had employed this device on two occasions prior to the construction of the library. Among the documented works of Mills one finds stairways disposed in this manner in both the State Insane Asylum erected in Columbia (1821–1828) and in the Marine Hospital which was built in Charleston during the years 1831–1834. Based upon the diary drawings, the character of the reading room, the facade and the treatment of the stairs, we may conclude that the new College building was composed as a pastiche; it included elements of several designs by Robert Mills. Exactly how this came to be is another matter. We can only hope for the discovery of further documentary evidence which will focus our observations and give credit to all of those who collaborated in the creation of the South Caroliniana Library.

Perhaps one reason that there are gaps in our knowledge of the Caroliniana is that the project was completed without complications. There is no body of memoranda about the library, for example, comparable to the controversy surrounding Richard Clark and the construction of Rutledge and DeSaussure Colleges. The surviving documents suggest that the building of the library was a pleasant experience for the Board. Little more than a year after the signing of the contract with Charles M. Beck, the Board was able to request of the legislature "an appropriation of $3436.23 to complete the Library Hall." This request was successful, and within six months, on 6 May 1840, President Barnwell informed the Trustees that the building was complete and in use.

The Final Buildings

Harper and Legare Colleges, the Observatory, Miscellaneous Restorations and the College Hall

1840-1855

The western extensions of the Horseshoe were defined by the completion of Lieber College in 1836 and the Library in 1840. Between 1840 and 2 December 1863, when the campus was closed "as a matter of necessity," the Trustees initiated a number of architectural projects.[1] Harper and Legare Colleges, both built in 1848, and the new observatory, which was finished in 1852, provided new academic facilities. Rutledge and DeSaussure Colleges were renovated after disastrous fires in 1855 and 1851 respectively. The first and second-built faculty houses were also reconstructed in the mid-1850s, and with several of these projects under way, work began in 1852 on the elaborate new chapel, or College Hall, which is now called Longstreet. This final period in the development of the College is notable, for much of its activity reflects a new level of architectural ambition, stylistic aspirations which were first evident in the reading room of the new library and which culminated in the new College Hall. A number of professional architects contributed to the growth of the institution during these years, and in their participation we see reflected the shifting tastes of the times.

The exuberant compositions which Edward Brickell White (1806–1882) proposed for the College demonstrate the passing of the Greek Revival and the advent of a romantic eclecticism. We have remnants of two suggestions which E. B. White made to the Trustees. The earlier of these, a drawing of a gate lodge to stand at the head of the Horseshoe (Figure 47), is undated. There was discussion among the Trustees of the need for such a building during the 1840s, and we may assume that White, who was working in Charleston, submitted his idea in response to these discussions. Be that as it may, the factors that prompted his design did not impede his imagination. In his carefully rendered wash drawing, we see the dome of Saint Peter's Cathedral superimposed upon what is basically a Roman triumphal arch. The intended utility of this architectural omelette is seen in the carriage which is passing through the

[1] Trustees' minutes, 2 December 1863.

FIGURE 46 *left*. "New Chapel and Exhibition Hall, and Halls for the Euphradian and Clariosophic Societies, So Ca College, E. B. White, Architect," no date, from the collection of the South Caroliniana Library.

FIGURE 47 *above*. The Porter's Lodge, College of Charleston, 1852, by E. B. White, from a photograph by Robert M. Smith, Photo-Vision, Columbia.

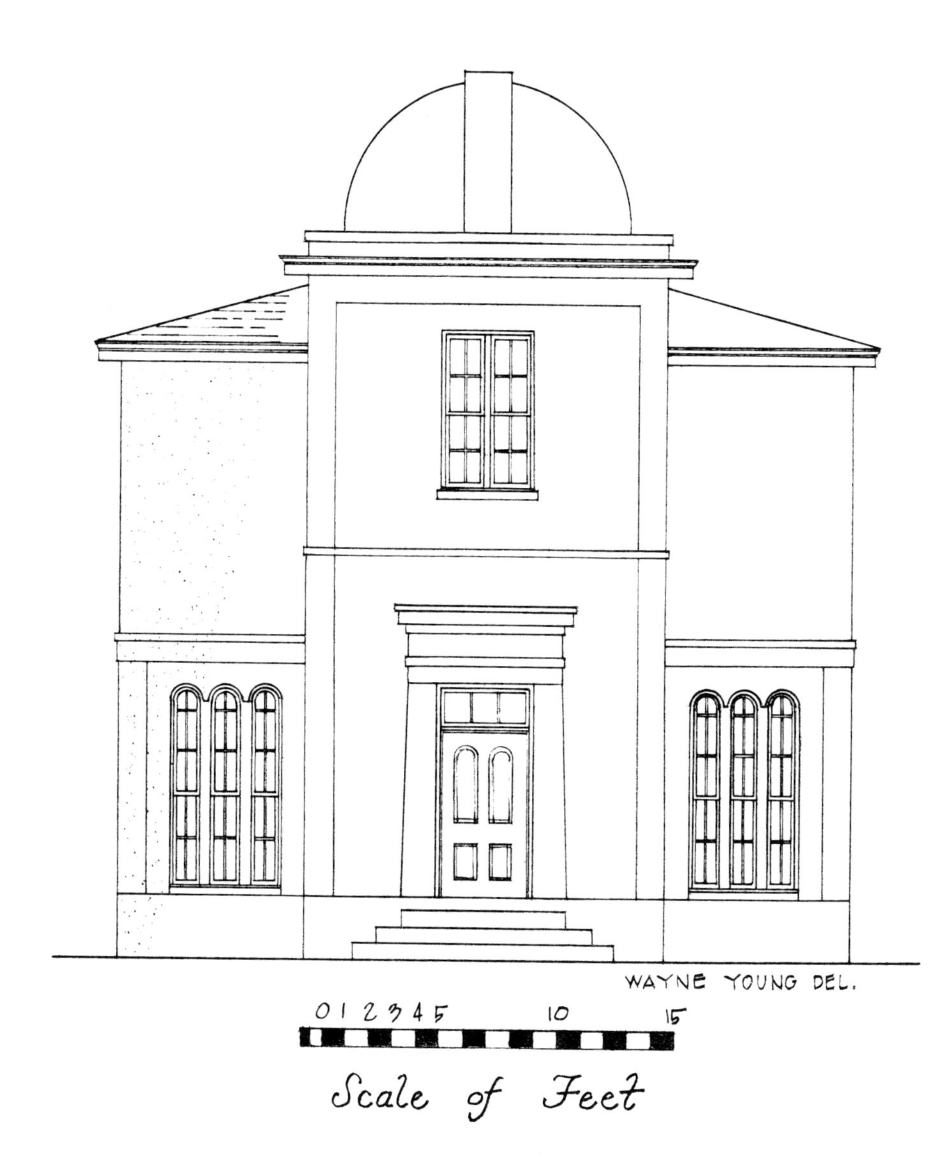

FIGURE 48. The Observatory, a reconstruction: research by John Califf, drawing by Wayne Young.

archway and by the windows seen in the upper level. The upper level was designed to provide an assembly room for the literary societies of the College. There is no record of the Trustees' reaction to this proposal; perhaps they did not deign to discuss it. In any case, monies were never appropriated for such a structure. These efforts by E. B. White were not wholly fruitless, for a similar building, albeit without the dome (Figure 48), was erected to his design at the College of Charleston in 1850.[2]

Other proposals by E. B. White are contained in a letter which he addressed to the Chairman of the Executive Committee of the Board of Trustees:

Hon W. C. Preston Charleston May 1st 1846

Sir:

Herewith I have the honour to present plans for refitting the Chapel, and improving the residence and premises of the President's House of South Carolina College Columbia.

The plans for the chapel contemplate stripping the entire interior of the present Chapel, laying a new floor, putting in new doors, and windows, removing the north end and extending the apartment 36 feet in that direction. The plans explain the projected arrangement. The center of the apartment is divided from the sides by two rows of fluted Roman Corinthian columns surmounted by an entablature highly enriched from which springs a coved ceiling which is broken into deep panels with a rosette in the bottom of each panel. The ceiling is further ornamented by three rich stucco centers surrounded by an embellished border. At the north end opposite the door of entrance is a platform raised upon three steps with a lower platform on each side and behind is a semicircular recess the floor of which is encompassed with fluted corinthian pilasters raised two steps higher; supporting a coved and panelled ceiling such as already described, with a lantern in the crown to admit light. At the north end the faculty and Trustees will be seated on the lowest platform, the stand for the orator will be on the next higher, and on the upper most platform the President of the College accompanied on public occasions by the Governor and Lieut Governor of the State, the Speaker of the House and President of the Senate. On each side of the apartment behind the columns is a commodious and elegant gallery for the accomodation of spectators. The main floor of the Chapel is occupied with benches having handsome carved sycamore ends as shown by the section. The staircase which now passes through the chapel to be removed and access to be had to the apartments above the Chapel by the nearest staircase in the west wing of the College; by making a passage between two rooms in the 3rd story of that wing from the head of that staircase to said apartments. The benches of the Chapel upon the main floor contain 390 seats, in the galleries 180 seats. Total 570 seats and a bench may be made against the walls of the galleries to contain 76 seats more, the cost for the foregoing will be $8000.

. . . .

I have Sir the honour to be with the highest respect your
very obet servt Edw. B. White
Architect[3]

The proposals concerning the College Chapel sprung from the need for a large assembly room. This need, as we will see, was discussed for some time, and the Trustees concluded that the extension of the existing Chapel as proposed by White would not provide the space required by the College. In this context, White's letter may be viewed as one element in the ultimate decision to undertake the construction of the new College Hall. More significantly in this letter, as in the drawing of the gate lodge, we have evidence of the ornamental architecture considered by the Board of Trustees during the last phase of the development of the College.

[2] Ravenel, *Architects of Charleston*, 183–202, presents the most extensive published treatment of the work of E. B. White.

[3] Miscellaneous File. SCL.

It would be a mistake to assume that the proposals by E. B. White were rejected simply because they were ornate. Indeed, the Trustees' affinity for ornament became plain when they determined to build a separate building to serve as a chapel, for then they chose the most elaborate design ever built by the College. It is also interesting to note that when the central block of Rutledge burned in 1855, Jacob Graves (— –1856) was retained to design the reconstruction. His design incorporated many of the elements of the chapel earlier proposed by E. B. White. The Trustees did not eschew ornament, but we must not present the development of the College as a chronicle of aesthetically significant projects.

At any given time during the life of the institution there were a number of utilitarian facilities under way. It is proper to touch upon some of these before treating the elaborate new College Hall. For example, among the documents relating to the maintenance of the institution we find a bill from "T. H. Wade and Tho Davis" "for building two privees of brick 14 x 16 feet in length and bredth finding all materials $650.00." These communal privees served Harper and Legare Colleges.

In another instance we can learn something about the cooking arrangements of the professors' families from the letter which William Hooper, Professor of Latin and Greek, wrote to the Trustees complaining that

> . . . my family is subject to much inconvenience and discomfort from the kitchen being in the basement of the dwelling house. The chimney smokes very badly and the fumes of cookery are diffused over the house even to the chambers above. A cooking stove was bought to prevent the fire place from smoking, but that has not proved a remedy. I submit to the Board whether they will think proper to build a kitchen at a suitable distance. I have consulted a carpenter and the estimated expence is about $150. If to this improvement were added that of fitting up the present kitchen for a dining room, it would materially promote the comfort of the establishment. This last change would cost something like $30 or $40.
>
> Very respectfully
> W. Hooper[4]

The bill of Thomas Wade tells us that this work was done and was certified as having been completed to Mr. Hooper's satisfaction on 30 October 1841.

A more ambitious, but nonetheless utilitarian, project was the construction of two new dormitory and classroom buildings—Harper and Legare Colleges—in the late 1840s. Dr. Edwin L. Green has succinctly expressed all that need be said about this undertaking.

> During the presidency of Hon. William C. Preston the number of students reached its maximum in ante-bellum days. In May, 1847, the professors were instructed to rent rooms in town for such students as could not be accommodated on the campus. A grant of $20,000 was secured from the Legislature to put up two new college buildings and remove the steward's house to the rear and south of the college buildings. President Preston reported in May, 1848, that the committee had contracted for two buildings, one connected with the old laboratory—Legare College—the other on the site of the Steward's Hall—Harper College—to be completed by October. They were meant to hold sixty students. The report of Dr. R. W. Gibbes for the building committee made in November shows that J. N. Scofield was the contractor, and that the cost was $20,543.82.
>
> In the center buildings of the two new colleges on the top floors were halls for the literary societies. An extra thousand dollars was spent in the fitting up of these. The Clariosophic Society moved into Legare College from its old home in Rutledge; the Euphradian Society, whose old quarters were in DeSaussure, occupied the uppermost floor of Harper College.[5]

[4] Hooper to Trustees, dated 3 January 1840. Miscellaneous File. SCL.
[5] Green, *History of the University*, 161.

Excepting the detailing in the rooms set aside for the literary societies, these buildings are wholly without architectural distinction. They are notable chiefly because they conformed to the dormitory ground plan established by Rutledge College, because they continued the frontage line along the mall and because as duplicates of one another, they maintained the mirror image effect which had begun with the placement of DeSaussure opposite Rutledge.

Other projects which affected the quality of life on campus included the introduction of running water into all the buildings in the mid-1840s, the installations of gaslights in 1857, and the modification of the fireplaces throughout the College in 1859 in order that coal might be burned instead of wood.[6]

The construction of a serviceable observatory was another of the notable utilitarian projects undertaken during this final phase of the development of the College. No record survives concerning the fate of the first observatory which had been completed in 1817. The second observatory (Figure 48), begun in 1851 and in use by May 1852, was the result of the efforts of Matthew J. Williams, Professor of Mathematics. His memoranda to Presidents William Campbell Preston and James H. Thornwell provide a glimpse of the influences which gave form to this highly specialized building.

Campus S. C. College
29 April 1851

Hon. Wm Preston
President S. C. C.

Dear Sir:

The trustees at their meeting in December last made two appropriations of $1200 each in favor of this Department of the College. One for the purchase of a telescope and the other for the erection of a building suitable to receive it. As soon as officially informed of these appropriations I renewed a correspondence previously opened with Mr. Henry Felz [?] Achromatic Telescope maker of N. Y. and finally closed a contract with him for the manufacture of an instrument of the following description viz:

1. Aperture of object glass 6¾ inches
2. Focal length 100 inches
3. Ten Eye-pieces—5 Huggenian [?] magnifying from 50 to 400 times and 5 Ramsden magnifying from 100 to 600 times
4. The whole to be mounted on Equatorial stand with clock-work to move the telescope
5. Hour circle 7 inches diameter—Declination circles 9½ inches di
6. The Finder, with an aperture of 2 inches to be a tolerable comet seeker
7. The whole packed and put on board of any vessel I may designate for the sum of $1200

In this contract you will perceive, I have neglected to provide for the expense of getting the instrument to Columbia. This expenditure will consist of two items neither of which can be very large, viz. the insurance and the freight. I am informed, the Telescope and its apparatus will probably be finished by the last of May or the first of June. In relation to the Observatory I have not made the same progress. Something besides a good instrument is necessary to secure accurate Astronomical observations. The telescope must be well mounted in a convenient building. To make sure of this requisite I have addressed letters to scientific friends in different parts of the United States from whom I have received abundant and minute details upon the subject. I have studied besides Prof W. C. Bond's [?] description of the Observatory at Cambridge Massachusetts, printed in pamphlet and accompanied with numerous and accurate drawings. With these data and under my general directions Mr. Graves, an Architect, has furnished two plans. The first will cost $1400, two hundred more than the amount appropriated. The second about $1000. I beg leave to accompany my report with these plans and the specifications of the first. There are no specifications of the second plan, in as much as it

[6] A detailed history of the development of the utility systems of the College could be written from the documents in the SCL Miscellaneous Files.

will differ from the first in no respect but in wanting the wings. In convenience, in amplitude, in architectural beauty and effect, the building constructed upon the first plan would be so far superior to the one built upon the second, that I have ventured to delay closing a contract for either until I could ascertain the wishes of the Trustees.

Where shall we erect the Observatory? I know of no place within convenient reach of the Department except upon the vacant lot to the west of the Campus.

. . . .

I have the honor to be, very respectfully
your obt. sert
Mat. J. Williams[7]

Seven months later Professor Williams wrote to the president to inform him that

Since my last report . . . The telescope ordered by the Board has arrived. Its entire cost including insurance and freight is $1224,55 which falls within the appropriation. I have not deemed it advisable to unpack the instrument until the building intended for its reception shall have been completed. By the terms of the contract the Observatory ought to have been finished by the 15th of last Octr. The failure was not the fault of the contractor. The dome which surmounts the edifice revolves easily by means of five cannon-balls cast and ground to accurate spheres, moving in a grooved cast-iron track. This apparatus could not be obtained here, It was cast in Massachusetts. The delay in receiving this essential part of the work [*illegible*] for sometime the progress of the building. It is now rapidly hastening to its completion. The house and telescope will be ready for use in a short time.

The following spring, Professor Williams reported to James H. Thornwell, the new President of the College, that the Observatory was completed: " . . . in addition to the daily recitations in Astronomy the members of the Senior class have eagerly attended several hours of many nights in the Observatory to examine the heavens through the telescope. The Observatory is finished and the telescope mounted. I am happy to say the instrument fully answers the expectations I had formed of its power and finish."

Professor Williams goes on to note that there was only one minor problem with the new facility:

In the transportation from N. Y. to this place the clock work by which the axis of the telescope is made to conform to the diurnal revolution of the earth was deranged and to some extent injured. The injury is not capital and may, I find be repaired by the skill of our own mechanics. For this purpose I have employed a citizen of the town to refit the clock and can pay for the expense from the appropriation made by the Trustees at their last meeting for finishing & fitting up the Observatory.

With Great Respect
your obt serv
Matt. J. Williams[8]

Having completed the Observatory, Jacob Graves and Professor Williams began to campaign for the rehabilitation of the faculty residences. From the resulting correspondence there can be no doubt that the first pair of faculty houses had fallen into serious disrepair. Indeed, the oldest faculty house (built in 1805 on the site of the present President's House) was deemed to be unstable and was demolished in 1854; the second faculty house (McCutchen House, built in 1813) was renovated after much ado in 1855. The earliest evidence that something was afoot appears in a letter written by Jacob Graves on 23 January 1853, to Professors Maximilian LaBorde and Matthew Williams, the residents of McCutchen House.

[7] Miscellaneous File. SCL.
[8] Idem.

Columbia Jan 23rd 1853

Messers Dr. Laborde & Mat Williams,

Having, by your request, examined the Houses in which you live, I find that the side walls have sprung outward for the want of strength in the mortar, and it appears, this process of springing out is still going on, but, that the bonds of the masonry are not yet broken. This can be remedied by passing thru iron rods through the width of the building between the ceiling of the first and the floor of the second stories, fastened with suitable heads and nuts.

. . . .

very respectfully yours
J. Graves, Archt[9]

Only two days later Jacob Graves wrote another letter, pertaining to the first-built faculty house, and sent it to Robert Gibbes, then serving on the Executive Committee of the Board.

Columbia Jan 25th 1853

Dear Sir,

I have examined Mr. Pelham's house with a view to making it safe until the vacation.

I can but say, I think it in a very precarious condition. It *May* stand for years as it is, and yet I consider it liable to a crash at any moment.

Its security may be secured for the present, by drilling through the walls and spiking irons upon the flooring provided with nuts and screws upon the outside—taking care that opposite timbers be so secured and that the ends where they come together be tied by an iron strap—This can be done at a slight expence and the building made safe until it is convenient to make a thorough repair.

Very respectfully yours
J. Graves Archt[10]

It was the end of the year before the Trustees requested that Thomas Davis, a carpenter, and P. P. Hammarskold, architect, examine the state of the College buildings. In their report, dated 2 December 1853, they recommended minor repairs to the President's house, including "that the whole exterior of the building may be rough-cast or cemented." Concerning McCutchen, "the double brick building occupied by Messer Professors Laborde and Williams," they noted that it was

> much out of repairs . . . the backwall of the building is somewhat bent outwards, from causes arising from the settlement of interior parts and divisions of the building. To make this good, and fully secure against any further damage, it is respectfully proposed that a wing or central projection may be erected from the centre of the building in the rear, which wing would form a substantial abutment for the back wall and at the same time give a small room for each of the tenements
>
> . . . .
>
> The building the last mentioned lately occupied by Mess Pelham is, we must report to be in a miserable and delapidated state, both the interior and the exterior, and it is unfit for any repair.[11]

Despite this report, the Board did nothing as winter passed into spring. Professor LaBorde then solicited yet another statement from P. H. Hammarskold, the architect who had reported to the Trustees.

Professor C F. McCay
South Ca. College

Columbia May 3rd 1854

Dear Sir,

According to the request of yourself and Professor LaBord I have made a close estimate for the very necessary repair which is required in your dwellings, to make them secure and comfortable. I have included in the estimate the addition which you desire, in the rear of your buildings and which would give to each of your dwellings three additional rooms with fireplaces for all the rooms. The addition

[9] Idem.
[10] Idem.
[11] Idem.

would be constructed fully according to your suggestion and in the best workmanlike manner . . . the addition in the rear of the buildings would contain [*illegible*]. The said addition is also very much needed to give full strength to the old and dilapidated building as without that the rear addition is made, and a thorough repair performed, at an early moment on the whole of the building, I can hardly see how the building could escape meeting with the same fate as those opposite your dwellings, formerly occupied by Mess. Pelham and Reynolds

. . . .

truly your most obt etc
P. H. Hammarskold[12]

Dire predictions notwithstanding, the Board did not vote an appropriation for McCutchen House. The unhappy Mr. Williams resigned (due to ill health), and with Mr. Williams gone, Professor LaBorde and his new co-tenant, McCay, submitted a vivid statement of the situation to the Trustees on 28 November 1854:

Columbia Nov 28th 1854

The Hon. The Board of Trustees S. C. College

The undersigned would beg leave to call your attention to the condition of the house in which they now reside & to ask an appropriation with the view of making such improvements as are indispensable to the comfort of their families. A simple statement of facts we believe is all that is necessary to indicate the justice of our appeal. One of us is now entering upon his twelfth year in the college & has expended more in permanent improvements of his house & premises than was ever allowed him by the Board. The amount thus appropriated from his private purse is from six to eight hundred dollars. The tenement in which he resides has but six rooms, & but three of these can be used as chambers. He has a family of *ten* & the Board can well conceive the great discomfort & inconvenience to which he is subjected. The other tenement of course has the same number of rooms, & the professor who occupies it has a family of six. When it is added that he found some of these rooms in such a state as not to be habitable the floors of some being so rotten as to have given away, the plastering of others in a falling condition, & that nothing has been done by the Board to remedy the evil, we feel that the Hon. body will not hesitate to do what is so obviously proper and necessary.

To this we would add that we have much fewer accommodations than the other officers in the campus, & that the north wall of our house has bulged out between two & three inches, & that this yielding of the wall slowly increases from year to year so that our families are more or less alarmed for their security & safety, & so that several architects & builders who have been called to examine it have declared that unless a remedy is applied soon, it will be impossible to effect it at all.

The undersigned have digested a plan for improving their house which plan has been approved by all the builders of the town as sufficient to prevent any farther damage to the building. It contemplates an addition of three rooms to each tenement & unites the advantages of cheapness & convenience. We have had an estimate made of the cost of these new rooms & of the plastering & other repairs needed in the present building & find that the whole can be done for less than half the cost of the new house erected on the opposite side of the campus.

The undersigned know not the condition of your treasury, but in their desire to have the work done as speedily as possible, they would respectfully press your body to anticipate in part the funds accruing in October if it be necessary. With a small advance payment it is confidently believed that the larger amount may, by contract be postponed until October without increasing the cost of construction.

In conclusion we would ask the appointment of a committee in view of having the matter in fuller detail brought before you.

With the highest regard Gentlemen
we are your most obdt
M. Laborde
C. F. McCay

[12] Idem.

PS
Since writing the above we have consulted Mr. Niernsee—Architect of the State Capitol—on our building after examination he declared that the back wall had bulged out two or three inches, & that the injury was slowly increasing & added that the new walls proposed, by acting as buttresses—would effectually prevent all further damages
C. F. McCay

In the spring of 1855 the repairs and additions sought by Professors Williams, LaBorde, and McCay were begun. This work established the basic elements of McCutchen House as it stood at the outset of the 1974–1976 restoration. The letters of the professors concerning McCutchen note the "fate" of the opposite residence "formerly occupied by Mess. Pelham and Reynolds." This, of course, was the first faculty house. In 1854 it was judged to be dilapidated and irreparable. It was thereupon demolished and replaced by the buildings currently used as the home of the President of the University (Figure 49). Although none of the drawings survive for this fourth double faculty residence (that was its intended use), extensive contracts and specifications have been preserved. Judged as narrative, this material is banal, but it richly compensates the reader by presenting the minutiae of the building trades in Columbia at midcentury. All of these documents are presented here.

State of South Carolina, City of Columbia

Articles of agreement made and concluded the 17th day of February A.D. eighteen hundred and fifty four by and between Dr. J. H. Thornwells, R. W. Gibbes & W. F. DeSaussure, being a majority of the Executive Committee, for the Trustees of South Carolina College, and Clark Waring Contractor for the building of two three story brick tenement Dwelling Houses for South Carolina College.

1. The said Clark Waring agrees for the consideration hereinafter mentioned, to perform in a good and workmanlike manner, under the direction of P. H. Hammarskold Archt. (or the Archt. for the time being) all the work mentioned and shown in the Specifications and Plans hereunto annexed and identified by the signatures of the parties hereto, to give his personal superintendence and attention to the same, and to provide at his own expense proper and sufficient materials therefor, according to the true intent and meaning of said Specifications and Plans: and in case any particulars shall be deficient, or not clearly expressed in said Specifications and Plans, the said Clark Waring will carry out the general design *as directed by the said Architect* in as thorough a manner as if the same were fully expressed.

And in case any of said work or materials, done or provided by the said Clark Waring shall be unsatisfactory to the said Architect, the said Clark Waring will, on being notified thereof by the said Architect, immediately remove such unsatisfactory work or materials, and supply the place thereof with other work and materials satisfactory to the said Architect P. H. Hammarskold.

2. It shall be lawful for the said Executive Committee at all times to direct in writing any additions to or deviations from the specifications aforesaid, without in any other respect or particular varying this agreement or impairing the force thereof, and in case of any such deviation or addition so directed in writing, such further time shall be allowed for the completion of the said work as the said Architect and the said Executive Committee shall decide to be reasonable, and such sums of money shall be added to or subtracted from the amount of the consideration hereinafter agreed to be paid as the said Architect and the said Executive Committee shall judge the increase or diminution in the amount of work and materials thereby occassioned, to be fairly worth.

3. In case of any failure or unreasonable delay of the said Clark Waring whether by act or default, in the performance of any of the above stipulations, or in compliance with the true intent of these presents, not authorized in writing by the said Executive Committee it shall be lawful for the said Architect P. H. Hammarskold (or the Architect for the time being) after ten days notice in writing to the said Clark Waring to provide other workmen and materials to complete the said work in the place of the said Clark Waring, and to deduct the cost and charges thereby occasioned, from the sums other-

FIGURE 49. The President's House, from a photograph by Judith Steinhauser.

wise becoming due to the said Clark Waring, under this agreement, without prejudice to any other remedy which the said Executive Committee or the Legislature of South Carolina may have for breach thereof.

4. The said Dr. H. H. Thornwell, R. W. Gibbes & W. F. DeSaussure, a majority of the Executive Committee for the Trustees of South Carolina College, in behalf of the State of So. Ca. agree to pay to the said Clark Waring the sum of Eleven Thousand Dollars ($11,000) in money, and also the two old three story brick tenement dwelling houses (now standing and being on the same lot where the new building is to be erected). The payments in money to be made in the following manner, to wit: Four Thousand Dollars ($4,000) when the work commences, Two Thousand Dollars ($2,000) when the joists are laid for the principal story floor, Two Thousand Dollars ($2,000) when the house is covered in, and the balance or Three Thousand Dollars ($3,000) when the whole of the work is finished, and accepted by the said Architect P. H. Hammarskold, as complete in every respect and manner to the entire satisfaction of said Architect and the said Executive Committee as fully meeting their views and expectations. The Payment aforesaid to be made on certificates signed by the said architect P. H. Hammarskold (or the architect for the time being.)

5. The said Clark Waring agrees well and truly to perform and finish all the matters and things contained in this contract and by him undertaken to be done, according to the terms of this contract, and the specifications, Plans and Instructions referred to in this contract, and that the same shall be completed on or before the first day of September in the year of Our Lord 1854. The whole work and every part thereof to be completed to the entire satisfaction of the Architect and of the Executive Committee of the Trustees of the South Carolina College as meeting their views and expectations in every respect and manner, and at all times subject to the rejection or approval of the said Architect.

Signed sealed & delivered
in presence of
P. H. Hammarskold
Ralph E. B. Stevenson

J. H. Thornwell
W. F. DeSaussure
R. W. Gibbes
Clark Waring

Specifications, for building two three story brick tenement dwelling houses for the South Carolina College.

The specifications will be written so as to describe and specify only one of the above named tenement brick buildings, but it is nevertheless to be well understood that the proposals are to be given for the two tenement dwelling-houses as shown on the Plan.

Location The building is to be located on a lot belonging to the College of So. Ca. (as will be shown and directed by the Architect) on the south line of what is generally called "The Campus."

Dimensions and General Description To be in every respect according to the Plans and Dimensions marked thereon (or to be found according to a scale of 1/8 of an inch to the foot applied to the designs.) The front of the building to have one principal entrance door, with exterior porch and steps to lead to the entrance hall; the porch to have 2 turned columns, with their bases and caps, as per detail design, also corresponding pilasters and entablature, the whole to be painted with three coats of best paint and sanded so as to resemble free stone. The platform and buttresses to be of brick and cemented in such manner, and colored as directed so as to resemble the other cemented work on the building as hereinafter described; one private entrance door to be also on the front, with steps leading into the front room of the basement story (marked study). The butresses and steps for this last named door to be built like those steps before mentioned. The trimmings around all the exterior doors to be of wood, painted and sanded as aforesaid; the exterior doors to be grained as hereinafter described all the trimmings exteriorly around windows as shown on the design, to be in cement and colored, as all other cementing. The sills under windows to be of pine, 5 inches thick, painted and sanded as above named exterior woodwork; the blocks used under the window sills, (wherever shown on the plans) to be of terra cotta, they will be furnished the contractor by the architect at a cost of 62½¢ apiece. The cornice around the building to be brickwork and cement or of wood, (moulded as per design, and full size detail drawings, hereafter to be furnished the contractor) at the option of the contractor, if in cement it must be colored as all other cement-work, and if of wood the cornice must be painted and sanded as above named to immitate free stone & under the cornice, on the front of the building will be used terra cotta brackets, which the architect will furnish to the contractor at $5 apiece. The division brick wall between the two tenement buildings to be run up through the roof as shown on the designs so as to prevent communication from one dwelling to the other in case of fire, the terra cotta ornaments to be painted two coats and sanded like the exterior woodwork. Part of the rear of the building to have piazzas (to extend between the projecting wings of the two tenements) as shown on the designs. The piazzas to be for all three stories with pointed brick piers for the basement story and with turned columns for the upper story's, the caps and bases of the brick piers to be cemented mouldings. The piers, and all that part of the exterior brick walls which are in the piazzas to be whitewashed. From the plans and elevations is seen all the exterior construction not before mentioned.

The Basement Story, to contain a hall with principal entrance door & with private door leading out to the side of the building under the staircase, a small closet under the stair-case, and the principal staircase leading to the second or principal story; The basement story contains also 3 rooms viz. a study, a breakfast-parlour, and a gentlemans private room as shown on the plan of said story with all the doors and windows and one fireplace for each room according to said plan, and the dimensions marked thereon a piazza is on the rear of this story with doors to the breakfast and gentlemans private room. The basement story is 2 feet above the level of the ground and is 10 feet high in the clear.

The Principal Story will contain a hall, a front parlor, a back parlor and a chamber a staircase in the hall to lead to the third story; there are to be large sliding doors between the two parlors and fire-places in each of the three rooms above-named. The principal story is 13 feet high in the clear and is to be neatly finished in every respect. There is also a piazza in the rear of this story all the doors and windows to be as per plans.

The Third Story contains a hall a bedroom a nursery, a chamber, and a small dressing or bathing room, and a piazza in the rear. There are fireplaces in the bedroom the chamber and in the nursery all windows and door openings to be as marked on the plans, a trap door is to be in the ceiling of the hall or corridor leading up to the garret.

The Garret is to contain no division or closets except specially agreed upon; a trap door is to be on the roof 2.6″ x 3′ on the rear side of the roof. The third story is to be ten feet high in the clear. The whole to be in full accordance with plans, and the following specifications and as hereafter instructed by the architect and more fully seen from detail drawings whenever such may be desired by the contractor.

Excavations earth to be excavated to receive all the foundations. The earth therefrom to be graded around the buildings as the architect may direct when the building is completed all surplus soil and refuse materials to be removed from the ground.

Brickwork all to be done with best Columbia bricks and mortar of fresh stone lime and clean sharp sand or gravel and to be laid in a good and workmanlike manner. The foundations to be at least 2.6″ deep under the surface of the ground or more if the nature of the ground should require. The foundations are to be 1½ feet wider at the bottom than the thickness of their respective walls (according to the plan of the basement story) and racked up to the thickness of the wall where the floor joists are laid all foundations for the chimneys for the piers of the piazza and for the steps etc. to be built in a substantial and proper manner.

The exterior walls of the building are to be of the following dimensions, to wit, the front wall of the basement story 2½ the side walls as far back as to the wings (to be 2 bricks thick all the other walls of the basement story to be 2 bricks thick all the exterior walls for the two upper storys to be 1½ bricks in thickness and the entire division wall between the two tenements to be 1½ bricks thick from top to bottom (with foundations as aforesaid) The piers under the piazza to be built 2 bricks square (1.6″) pointed and whitewashed as aforesaid. The three chimney stacks to be built in the best manner and as shown on the plans (two of them to be common to both tenements) with separate flues well [*illegible*] and not less than 14 inches square for each fireplace. The stacks to be topped out (as shown on the elevation) and roughcast; all air holes to be made when required. All the exterior brick-work to be pointed, (except when other-wise specified to be cemented or whitewashed). Flat arches to be over all window and door openings.

The Mortar for all the above work must be composed of fresh stone lime and sharp clean sand or gravel, in such proportion as will insure a strong and durable cement.

Cementing and Roughcasting, in addition to the cementing aforesaid, all the base around the building is to be cemented in the best manner, the cementing to come as low as 6 inches under the surface of the ground. The chimney tops, and that part of the division wall which is shown above the roof is to be rough-cast in the very best manner all the cementing to be colored as directed by the architect so as to resemble free stone.

Carpenter Work. The floor joists in all the storys to be 3 by 10 inches except the joists over the third story which may be 3 by 9 inches all the joists to be 16 inches between centers with a row of solid bridging through the center of all the rooms and halls. The floors to be of yellow Southren pine boards 1¼ inch thick from 6″ to 8″ wide planed tongued and grooved and secret nailed, free from sap large or loose knots and to be smoothed off after they are laid. The floor boards to be picked for the principal story for the halls and for piazzas (the basement story Piazza is to be paved with bricks) All the steps in front of the basement story doors under the piazza to be of wood with nosings, (all the exterior basement story steps and their buttresses to be built of bricks & cemented as aforesaid.)

Partitions all the partitions of the building to be studded with scantling 3 by 4 inches except those at the doors which are to be 3 by 6 inches all to be placed 16 inches between center and center & set 3 inches and strongly nailed at the floor and ceiling the roofs and floors of the piazzas to be framed with lumber of such sizes as are requisite and all other framing to be done which may be necessary for the completion of the building in a good and workmanlike manner with necessary *foundations* for partitions.

The Ceilings of the Piazzas are to be lined with ¾ inch yellow pine boards well seasoned and to be quartered beaded and grooved together with white lead in the joints & smoothed off for painting.

The Piazza Columns for the principal & third storys to be turned out of well seasoned pine with square plinths, and caps in the doric order without ornaments according to detail drawings the entablatures of the piazzas to be plain Tuscan moulded, the rails between the columns and the ½ pilasters of the piazzas to be common square hand rails with capping and square balusters in the usual manner. All to be put up in a good and workmanlike manner.

The wooden floors of the piazzas to be grooved together with white lead and strongly secret nailed.

Roof, the joists 3 by 9 inches to be placed 16" apart notched down to the wall plates 3 by 9 inches to protect 2 inches from the face of the wall and well bedded thereon

The rafters of thc roof are to be of the usual cut 3 by 8 inches and those in the vallies 3 by 9 inches all to be placed 24″ apart from center to center and closely sheated. The heels of the rafters to be framed into the joists and the whole framing of the roof with its principals king and queen posts braces etc put up and fastened in a substantial and workmanlike manner. The roof to be boarded with boards 1 inch thick the edges straight laid close and nailed to the rafters with nails on both edges and properly prepaired for shingling. The shingles to be good cypress shingles, not less than 5/8 of an inch thick in the but end, sawed, straight and out of wind the shingles to be not less than 18 inches long to be laid in a proper manner and nailed fast with 4 penny nails the shingles to show about 1/3 of its length (say 6 inches) the but ends to be laid in a straight line and the whole covering completed in a workmanlike manner so that no leakage may exist whatsoever.

Inside Dressing the washboards in the basement story rooms and in the entire third story to be 8 inches high including sub and 1 inch moulding at the top. The entrance hall and the entire principal story to have washboards 10 inches high including a 2 inch sub and 1½ inch moulding at the top The subs are to be firmly nailed to the floors.

Stair Cases, the main inside stairs to extend from the basement floor to the third floor 2 flights as shown on the plans. The steps and riser to be of clear yellow pine (southern) moulded tongued and grooved glued blocked, and secret nailed with [*illegible*] under nosings. Inside of stair case to have on one side vamped base (moulded as the washboards) with the ends of the steps housed wedged and glued all supported on proper carriages. The stair case to have 3 inch hand rails and 1½ inch turned balusters with a 5 inch newel with cap and base turned and octagon shaft all to be properly grained and varnished 3 times.

Windows to be as shown on the plans and of such size as marked thereon all the frames to be boxed frames and all the sashes to be divided into two runs with 6 lights in each run. (the lights to be of such size for the different parts of the building as they are marked in the plans) both the lower and the upper run of the sashes to be of Nim's Patent Sashes with springs as to slide easy up and down and the springs to properly resist the sash so that it may stop in any part of the frame. The sashes to be 1½ inch thick all the windows in the basement story rooms and in the third story to have plain heads and backs, with 6 inches wide architraves around all the said windows and the doors. All the windows in the principal story and in the basement story hall to have double architraves 8″ wide; around all the corresponding doors to be equal trimmings, and all the heads and backs of said windows and doors to be panelled in good style the dados under said windows to be recessed and panelled. The architraves around all windows to continue down to the washboards with a plain plinth (of the same height as the washboard) to rest upon.

Venetian Blinds. To be for all the windows of the building the blinds to have standing slats in two panels all to be finished in good manner and of well seasoned yellow pine hung and fastened in the best style.

Doors, The front entrance door in the basement story to be double faced panelled and moulded. The principal entrance door to be 2 inches thick all the other basement story exterior doors to be 1¾ inches thick. The entrance door to be hung by 4 by 4 best butt hinges and secured by an iron plate flush bolt and fine 8 inch mortice lock with night key all the other doors in the basement story rooms and in the third story to be 1½ inch thick double faced panelled hung and secured in the best manner with good proper mortice locks and mineral knobs all closet doors to be single faced 1 inch plain panelled and properly hung and fastened. All the doors in the principal story to be 1¾ inch thick double faced panelled moulded hung and fastened in a fine style with best mortice locks and white mineral door knobs. The door knobs (and the bell knobs) for the principal entrance door to be white mineral knobs, and the trimmings on the lock to be silver-plated. The door between the front and the back parlour in the principal story to be double sliding door, to be 2 inches thick double faced panelled and moulded, to be furnished with best brass, steel bushed sheaves and brass ways inlaid in the floor. The doors to run easy and perfectly uniform and true, furnished with suitable mortice locks all the trimmings around the doors in the different story to correspond with their window trimmings.

Lathing all the interior of the buildings throughout to be lathed. The walls ceilings chimneys breasts soffits of staircase. The laths to be sawed and nailed to the furings with 3^{d} cut nails to be well butted up to each other and to break joints at every 14 inches as is usual. Space to be left between the laths for key at least ¼ of an inch no perpendicular laths to be nailed between the buts and at least 4 nails to be used for each lath and no lath to be used for which has large knots sapstain or bark which may discolor the plasterers work.

Plastering, In the halls of the basement story and of the principal story to be three coats of plastering in the following manner first and second coat to be of good lime mortar with proper proportions of clean fresh slaughtered hair the sand to be of a coarse description in the second coat than in the first coat and to be composed of two parts sand with one part Thomaston Lime the work to be properly plumbed and straightened throughout hand floored and trowelled up to a good finished surface all angles to be filled out square and true in the second coat.

Cornices and Mouldings are to be filled out with hair mortar to within one quarter of an inch of the finish and no greater thickness of lime and plaster to be used in filling out the cornices and mouldings the filling out to be gauged with ½ Plaster of Paris. All of the basement story (except the hall) and all of the third story to be plain finished with two best coats of Plastering with hard finish in a neat and workmanlike manner. The basement story hall and the principal story hall to have a small moulded cornice and a center flower of neat pattern in the ceiling (2½ or 3 feet in diameter) The two parlors in the principal story to have moulded stucco cornice of 16 inches girt and a neat center flower in the ceiling not less than three feet in diameter of approved pattern the chambers in the principal story to be finished with a small stucco cornice and a center flower like the halls.

Mantle Pieces The two parlours and the principal story chambers to have finely constructed and finished mantle pieces of cypress, or yellow pine all the other fire places to have plainer neat mantles of same material all to be in a style to be approved of by the architect or according to designs furnished by him. All the mantles to be painted and varnished as directed by the architect. The three fire places in the principal story to have blue stone hearths (which will be furnished to the contractor for about 16 dollars for the three fire places if the contractor should so desire) the other hearths throughout the building to be laid with brick and cemented over.

Iron Work All licks hinges fastenings &c for doors windows sashes shutters &c to be provided and put up in a good substantial and workmanlike manner all to be of such sizes and shape as will suit the purpose. *A Lightning Rod* to be put up at each of the two chimneys stacks in the division line for the two tenements to be arranged in all respects upon the most approved principle. Tinning to put tin in valleys & around chimney stacks whenever required five inch gutters to be put up under the eaves of the shingles inside of the parapet of brick-work and leaders to be put up to carry the water from the gutters outside of the building all the tinwork to be painted properly and cementing to be done when required to make the whole completed and good.

Painting All the exterior woodwork and terra cotta work (before mentioned) to be painted with 3 coats of best lead and pure linseed oil and sanded so as to imitate Brown Stone (free stone). The venetian blinds to be painted three coats on the priming in an approved green colour all the sashes to be painted exteriorly 3 coats and in a dark brown colour. All the exterior doors to be grained in oil colour except the doors in the rear of the piazza which are to [*illegible*] plain colour. All the interior washboards in the halls and the principal story to be grained and varnished. The hand-rail and balusters of staircase to be grained and varnished all the mantlepieces to be painted so as to imitate marble and to be varnished. All the interior doors in the basement and principal storys to be grained and varnished as directed all other doors to be painted in plain colors as directed and varnished. The two sliding doors to be painted in white and all other interior trimmings as architraves, windows frames sashes etc. to be painted in white color with varnish in the last coat all to have three coats of best paint and [*illegible*] in a fine style. The white to be prime pure white lead and linseed oil (or as the architect may direct other colors may be used in place of the white.)

Glazing all sashes to be glazed with best American white glaze well bedded bradded and back puttied. The lights in the front windows to be of 2d quality American plate glass.

Bellhanging 4 bells to be hung one in the third story one in the principal story and two in the basement story with their proper fastenings. Wires mineral knobs & the bells to be placed as directed on the south side of the building and the mineral bell pullies or knobs to be placed one on the front door two more in the basement story two in the principal story.

The State of South Carolina
City of Columbia

Know all men by these presents that we Clark Waring, Wm Maybin, T. J. Goodwyn, are held and firmly bound unto the State of South Carolina in the penal sum of twenty two thousand dollars ($22,000) to the payment of which well, and truly to be made, we bind ourselves, and each, and every of us, our heirs, executors, and administrators, jointly, and severally, firmly by these presents, seald with our seals, and dated this 16th day of February anno Domini one thousand eight hundred and fifty four.

Whereas, the above bound Clark Waring has this day made and entered into a contract in writing, under seal, with the State of South Carolina, through, and by the Executive Committee of the Trustees of South Carolina College Dr. J. H. Thornwell, R. W. Gibbes, & W. F. DeSaussure, being a majority of the said committee, to build and finish in a complete and workmanlike manner the two three story brick tenement dwelling houses, to be located on the south side of the College Square (or Campus) in the aforesaid State of South Carolina, as set forth and specified in the said contract and in Plans, Drawings, Schedules, and Specifications by P. H. Hammarskold, Architect.

Now the condition of the above obligation is such that if the above bound Clark Waring shall truly and well perform all the matters and things in said contract contained, and by him undertaken, to be done according to the terms of said contract, and the Plans, Drawings, Schedules and Specifications referred to in the said Contract, within the time in the said contract specified, and shall do the same under the direction and supervision of P. H. Hammarskold Architect, as in said contract specified, and shall refund to the said committee any advances which may have been made to the said Clark Waring on account of the said contract, in the event that he shall fail to perform the same in conformity with its stipulations, then and in that case the above obligation to be void and no effect, and it is agreed and stipulated that the said Clark Waring shall pay to the said State of South Carolina for each and every breach of his said contract the sum of fifty dollars as the stipulated measure of damages sustained by the said State of South Carolina, by and for such breach and the sum of five dollars per day for every day he shall be employed on said work beyond the day fixed for its completion, and that the penalty above mentioned shall stand as security for the payment for all such stipulated damages.

Signed sealed and delivered in presence of

P. H. Hammarskold	Clark Waring
Ralph E. B. Stevenson	Sm Maybin
	T. J. Goodwyn[14]

We may assume that the work was satisfactorily completed prior to 2 December 1854, when P. H. Hammarskold presented his bill to the Trustees.

As we have noted, the final phase of the development of the College saw the completion of two new "colleges," a new professors' residence, an observatory, and the extensive rehabilitation of the existing buildings. Important as these projects were, they were completely overshadowed by the major undertaking of the time—the construction of the New College Hall. E. B. White had proposed to enlarge the chapel in Rutledge College in 1846; his suggestion was apparently ignored. Two years later a petition was submitted to the legislature by "the Chaplain and Students of South Carolina College":

December 5th 1848

To the Honorable, the Senate, and house of Representatives, now met, and sitting in General Assembly;

The humble petition of the Chaplain and Students of the South Carolina College showeth, that the Hall which is appropriated to religious worship and to publick exhibitions is altogether inadequate to these purposes, both from the insufficiency of its accomodations and the uncomfortableness of its arrangements. At commencement yesterday it is estimated that not more than one fourth of the persons who were anxious to be present could be admitted into the building. Many of your own body were excluded and of those who obtained admission, many were compelled to stand during the whole exercises. On last Sunday, it is supposed that at least one hundred persons came to the door, and retired in consequence of the impossibility of being comfortably seated. It deserves to be mentioned, too, that since October last, the chapel has been found inadequate to accomodate the students at morning and evening prayers without introducing changes which may be productive of disorder. We add finally that the impression of strangers, in regard to us, are very much influenced by our Publick Halls. The first thing for which they enquire is our chapel, and we confess, that we are ashamed to show it. Harvard, Yale and Princeton can point with pride to the accomodations which their friends have made, for all who would attend, at their high festival.

These facts are submitted to your Honorable Body, whose liberal patronage, we have always experienced, in the hope that the pressing necessities of the case may lead to some measures to remove these evils. And your petitioners will ever pray & etc.[15]

[14] Idem.
[15] SCAH.

The legislature was not moved by the prayers of the student body. One year later, on 17 December 1849, when the legislature did pass a "Preamble and Resolutions directing the manner in which repairs shall be made to the S. C. College and as to building a new Chapel," the provisions of the Resolutions were not those sought by the students. Speaking of the Chapel in the Preamble, the legislators made it plain that "it is desirable that the same should be constructed without appropriations from this Legislature." While considering the subject of the building funds of the College, the legislators went on to resolve for good measure:

> That the Trustees of said College be required to cause all contracts for repairs or buildings and for supplies for said institution, where the same shall exceed one hundred dollars to be let to the lowest bidder, due public notice having first been given, and that the Treasurer shall in each annual report insert the names of all bidders, and the amount of each bid, and shall also state the specific object for which all money's paid by him have been expended.
>
> Resolved 2. That the said Trustees be earnestly requested to use all possible economy consistent with the preservation of the buildings and the comfort and health of the inmates of said institution, in order to raise a fund as soon as possible, to build a new chapel adapted to the wants of the institution, and the convenience of the public.[16]

Perhaps the criticism implicit in these resolutions was justified. The legislators must have remembered the additional monies required to complete the new library, not to mention the penchant of the Trustees to consume appropriations in the building of an unfinished shell, an expediency that had been employed in the construction of DeSaussure, the Library and Science building, and the lower story of the South Caroliniana Library. On the other hand, the legislators must have known that it would be impossible to fund a building through use of the tuition monies—the history of the professors' houses had already demonstrated the futility of this stratagem. It is interesting to note the "Report of the committee on the part of the Senate appointed to meet a similar committee from the House, to enquire and report on the expediency of enlarging the college Chapel or erecting a new one," a report made following the commencement exercises of 1851, for here the self-interest is baldly apparent that finally prompted the appropriation to build the chapel.

> . . . your committee have come to the conclusion that the present chapel is entirely too small to afford adequate accommodation for the members of the Legislature and patrons of the institution at the usual exhibitions of the college. At the late commencement a majority of the Legislature and a large number of visitors interested in the young gentlemen who were graduated, were excluded from the chapel for the want of room. Your committee believe that to enlarge the old chapel would be dangerous and would probably cost more than would be requisite to erect a new building, and therefore recommend the adoption of the following Resolution:
>
> Resolved, that the Board of Trustees of the South Carolina College be authorized to erect a new chapel for the college provided, that they shall not call on the state for more than ten thousand dollars to aid in the construction of the same.[17]

With the appropriation in hand, the Trustees determined the following spring "that a special committee be appointed to be charged with the duty of having a chapel erected at such site and upon such plan as they shall approve. . . ." This committee, which was composed of Governor Means, Mr. Preston, Mr. Adams, R. W. Gibbes, D. L. Wardlaw, J. J. Evans and John Buchanan, was directed to spend between $20,000 and $24,000 on the building. No records have survived from the first meeting of this committee; however, they must have convened at once, settled on a plan and

[16] Idem.
[17] Idem., 15 December 1851.

FIGURE 50. Longstreet, the College Hall, from a photograph by Judith Steinhauser.

advertised for bids, for on 19 July 1852, they held their second meeting, "and the following bids were offered for the work."

Killian and Fry $31,000
P. J. Suder and S. P. Welch $23,000
J. Troy and T. H. Wade $23,450
J. H. Long $27,900
C. Beck $29,523

The contract was granted to "Suder and Welch on condition that William Adger be security for them," and "the location was unanimously ordered to be on Sumter St. fronting Green Street." Having decided upon the location of the building, the committee provided that "should Wm. Adger refuse within a week to be security for Suder and Welch, then the contract to be given to Troy and Wade. On motion of Judge Wardlaw it was ordered that Mr. Graves do prepare a contract with the contractors in accordance with the specifications, as ammended by the committee."[18]

Here for the first time the name of "Mr. Graves" is associated with the new College Hall. There can be no question that he was the architect of the new building, as the Reports and Resolutions of the legislature for 9 December 1853, note "by cash paid Mr. Graves for the plan and specifications of the new chapel," and again on 9 July 1855, "Jacob Graves, on account of his services as architect of College Hall—$300." Jacob Graves figures prominently in the final projects of the South Carolina College. He designed the College Hall and superintended its construction. He is largely responsible for Rutledge College as we know it today. It would appear that he designed, as a faculty house, the current President's House which stands upon the site of the earliest faculty residence. He also designed the second Observatory in 1851. Despite these activities, little is known about Jacob Graves. He apparently came to Columbia c. 1850 expressly to practice architecture. The earliest documentary evidence of his presence seems to be the contract for the College Hall which he signed as an agent for the Trustees on 13 August 1852. Shortly thereafter the local newspapers began to carry an advertisement that one could find "J. Graves, Architect and Civil Engineer, residence and office on Bull Street Between Blanding and Laurel Streets."[19]

The records of the College, the legislature and the office of the Governor demonstrate that from the summer of 1852 through the winter of 1856 Jacob Graves was working on architectural projects for the state. Then, in a document dated 24 March 1856, we find that "this will certify that it is my wish that E. G. Graves should Administrate upon the Estate of Jacob Graves Late of Richland District. [signed] Susan L. Graves."[20] Jacob Graves died without a will, and among the brief listing of his effects we find "1 sett drawing inst $40, 1 Transit inst $160, office Furniture $50." It must have been with this "1 sett of drawing instruments" that he laid out the College Hall (Figures 50 and 51).

The contract which Jacob Graves drafted at the direction of Judge Wardlaw has survived. This contract, however, was not made with the lowest bidders, Suder and Welch, for they were apparently unable to provide suitable bond; instead, James Troy and Thomas H. Wade entered into a contract to construct the New College Hall.

> Articles of agreement made and concluded the thirteenth day of August in the year of our lord one thousand eight hundred and fifty two between the Trustees of South Carolina College of the one part

[18] Idem., 19 July 1852.
[19] *The Tri-Weekly South Carolinian*, 1 March 1853.
[20] Records of the Richland County Probate Court, Box 44, Package 1087.

FIGURE 51. Longstreet, the College Hall, from a photograph by Judith Steinhauser.

and James Troy, and Thomas H. Wade, of Columbia S. C. carpenters of the other part, as follows

To wit:

The said Jas Troy and Thos H. Wade, for the considerations herein after mentioned, do jointly and severally covenant, promise, and agree, to and with the said Trustees, that they shall and will, by the first day of October in the year of our Lord one thousand eight hundred and fifty three well and truly erect, build, set up, and finish, in Columbia, S. C. a Building for a Chapel for the College, according to plans and specification by J. Graves, Archt. and adopted by a Committee of the Trustees with the understanding that the capitols of the outside columns and all the outside modillions, are to be of cast iron and the windows and door caps and sills to the basement are to be of granite fine tooled and the brick of the common size the whole to be finished under the supervision of the Architect and to his acceptance.

In consideration whereof the said Trustees convenant and promise to and with the said Jas Troy and Tho H. Wade well and truly to pay or cause to be paid the sum of four thousand dollars when the work shall be commenced. Ten thousand dollars when the Legislature shall pass the appropriation bill for that purpose and five thousand dollars when the walls are up and finished and the remainder four thousand four hundred and eighty dollars when the whole shall be completed.

To each and several of the foregoing articles each of the said parties bind themselves firmly by these presents, in witness whereof we have hereunto set our hands and seals this thirteenth day of August A. D. one thousand eight hundred and fifty two

Witness — James Troy
R. W. Gibbes — Tho H. Wade
J. Graves Agent for Trustees[21]

The "plans and specifications by J. Graves, Archt." have not survived, but records have survived which indicate that Troy and Wade came to rue the day that they agreed to build the College Hall "under the supervision of the Architect and to his acceptance." The cornerstone of the building was laid with some ceremony early in December 1852. It was not long before things began to go awry. The cost of building materials rose between 20 percent and 50 percent in Columbia during the spring and summer of 1852. The contractors felt that this problem, grave in itself, was exacerbated by the vagueness of the architect's initial specifications. Both of these problems are presented by the contractors in a piteous letter to Governor Manning, who was then serving as Chairman of the Committee for the College Hall

To his Excellency the Governor and Board of Trustees of South Carolina College

Permit us to make to you a statement of the amounts actually expended for the erection of the Chapel up to this date. The cost of materials in many instances have increased from twenty to twenty-five per cent and are still advancing. . . . These statements we make that you may judge of what use and purpose we have made with the funds which have been paid us on our contract. We have been driven to the necessity of finishing up other jobs to assist us in going on with this. One other statement we wish to make viz in as large a building as the Chapel the most judicious contractor would be mistaken in its cost where only ground plans and elevations were given, with a clause in the specifications (that plans were later to be furnished by the architect) Moreover the Corinthian Order being in many instances very plain and when carried to its fullest extent the most difficult and expensive of all the orders, its entablature and projections being larger than any except the Tuscan which is plain and simple in its construction, in carrying out this order on a building of the size of the Chapell, with extra embellishments and ornaments the architect might desire to put on, this building might be increased in its cost from one to ten thousand dollars, being entirely within his power to require under the Specified Clause. This building if carried out with some additions and alterations will be superior to any building of the kind in the

[21] Miscellaneous File. SCL.

state, or we might say in the southern states. All of which is respectfully submitted

Troy and Wade
Contractors[22]

Columbia May 6, 1854

Governor Manning and the Committee refused to simplify or to modify the design to suit the contractors. The work puttered along at a frustrating pace. Everyone connected with the project became pessimistic. An undated report to the Trustees by the "Committee on the College Hall" glumly notes

> Your committee lament to say that all their exertions, aided by the resolutions of your honorable body, have failed to prevent the delay of the contractors and the vexations and disappointment consequent thereon. There is every reason to doubt at this time, whether the contractors have the inclination and ability to go on to the completion of their contract, although the architect is of opinion the work which yet remains to be done under the original contract will not cost so much as the sum which remains to be paid upon the completion. Negotiations are now in progress. . . .[23]

And the architect wrote to the Governor:

> Dear Sir. The Hall has not progressed in its finish since your last meeting, so fast as was expected, The heavy work is nearly all done and if the contractors should put on a suitable force there is time to finish the contract by the first of October next. but to insure that, it is necessary that the force be put on immediately,
>
> . . . .
>
> I feel a great anxiety about its completion and hope measures will be taken to have it done in good time. The contractors assure me that it shall be done.
>
> Very Respectfully,
> J. Graves, Archt.[24]

And the Governor, as Chiarman of the Committee, wrote to the Board of Trustees that the Committee

> have been greatly disappointed at the tardy progress of the work—that in point of time the contractors have failed by more than twelve months to comply with their contract as to the completion and delivery of the building . . .
>
> . . . .
>
> The committee are of opinion that taking every thing into consideration, the wisest course for the board to adopt would be to allow Messrs Troy and Wade to complete the work, in consideration of the fact that they seem anxious now to do so, notwithstanding the certainty that the completion of the contract in accordance with the plans and specifications of the architect Mr. Graves, will be attended with considerable loss to them. Their securities however are good for any failure on their part to comply with the contract.
>
> Respectfully submitted
> J L Manning[25]

Troy and Wade were allowed to continue, but months passed and the work was incomplete. The commencement of 1854 was held in the Hall "with the full understanding that no acceptance or approval of any part of the work shall be thence implied." This was a wise stipulation, for it rained during the ceremony, and the roof leaked like a sieve. Troy and Wade ultimately defaulted on their contract which was then given to Mr. William Maybin.[26] On 1 May 1855 Jacob Graves wrote to Governor James H. Adams that the new contractor was proceeding satisfactorily. On 28 November

[22] Idem.
[23] Idem., 2 December 1854.
[24] Idem., 3 May 1854.
[25] Idem., no date.
[26] Idem., Jacob Graves to Governor Manning, 9 May 1853.

1855 the architect submitted to Governor Adams a final accounting of the cost of the College Hall. The full text of this ledger does not survive; however, the total cost appears to have been approximately $34,600.[27]

After the completion of the new chapel the building activities of the College virtually ceased for half a century. During this long quiessence the architecture of the South Carolina College mellowed undisturbed. The Horseshoe passively accrued associations and memories, its aura of dignity and patina of age. For successive generations of Carolinians the campus became part of the passage into maturity. The efforts of the early Trustees proved to be durable, and it is a concrete tribute to these men, and to the architects, Richard Clark, Robert Mills, Jacob Graves, P. H. Hammarskold and the anonymous designer(s) of the South Caroliniana Library that their buildings are cherished and continue to serve.

[27] Idem.

Appendix

Evidence of Benjamin Henry Latrobe's participation in the design competition is found in a letter signed by Latrobe and dated "Philadelphia Aprl. 17th, 1802." The only extant text of this letter appears to be a typescript copy in the collection of the South Caroliniana Library. This document presents several problems. Inasmuch as the salutation is a simple "Sir" we do not know to whom the letter was addressed. Drawings are mentioned in the body of the letter, but apparently these "fair sketches" have been lost. Finally, the acquisition records of the Caroliniana shed no light upon the provenance of the typescript, much less the whereabouts of the original. Despite these problems, the letter seems worthy of presentation here, for internal evidence strongly suggests that the typescript accurately reflects an important document in the history of the College.

Philadelphia Aprl. 17th, 1802.

Sir,

I am highly flattered by your polite letter of the 14th currt. and if anything could induce me to enter into such a competition as is proposed by the Advertisement of the trustees of the S. Carolina College, it would be the letter you have written to me. But there are reasons, which your politeness renders it proper for me to state to you, which have long prevented men who have a reputation to lose, and who do not absolutely depend upon a *chance* of business for support, from encountering the sort of rivalry which a public notice calls forth. The merit of the design of a *professional* man of experience and integrity is, that nothing is proposed but what is *practicable*; *permanent*; *economical*, with a view to ultimate expenditure; & in point of taste, capable of encountering the severest criticism. But these are merits of which it is not easy for *unprofessional* men to judge *in a drawing*; & on that account the decission is not always according to the merits. I have now before me a most seductive design in point of drawing & coloring, & which has also some excellent points of arrangement, which has been submitted to me, to decide, whether it shall be executed or not. It is drawn by a most ingenious Amateur. But the chimnies cannot be carried up: the staircase has not head way enough by two feet, & lands so that the doors are inaccessible, & some of the upper walls have no support. These errors appear only on scrupulous examination, & no one was more surprised on discovery of them, than the designer. *Elegant*, but *impracticable* designs, which in their execution bring discredit on the art, are however not the only unpleasant rivals of those of professional men. Workmen, who are supposed to know more of expense & construction, than mere tasteful amateurs, are always deficient in arrangement. In private building their own *wants* & *habits* govern their plans of dwellings for gentlemen of quite different *wants* & *habits*; and in public buildings they generally have recourse to books. Excepting when books describe & delinate works of merit, actually executed, they generally have been published by men, whose want of business, & of experience, has given them leisure to speculate, & to build *castles in the Air*. Of this kind are almost *all* the books of Architecture with which I am acquainted, as Thomas's, Paine, Noan's, &c &c &c.—out of all which a judge of archirural merit, can gather valuable materials; but in which those, who usually have recourse to them, are incapable of distinguishing beauties from defects.

Having determined never to submit a plan to any public body which should not be so disgested in its minutest arrangements as to satisfy my own mind of its practicability, & eligibility; & which, in case of my death or absence, should not be sufficient to guide my successor to its perfect completion, I find it extremely inconvenient & humiliating to devote a month's time to making a complete set of drawings & calculations, & to collecting such information respecting the materials to be had, the contracts to be procured, & the expense attending them, as would authorise a risk of reputation, and this only for the *chance* of being preferred to the Amateur, & workmen who may enter the lists against me. It is the misfortune of our country, that in most instances men of natural genius, who have had little instruction, and less opportunity of improvement are preferred to men, who have expended the best part of their lives in endeavoring to acquire that knowledge which a good Architect & Engineer ought to possess. I have in all those instances, in which I have taken my chance with others, been thrown out by some such genius, & I have an habitual dread of them. They have, either as possessing the confidence of building committees, or holding a seat in the committee often made me repent that I have cultivated my profession in preference to my farm. And it is Because I have no means of preventing the inroads of these gentlemen upon the steadiness, the consistency, & energy of my system of operations, unless I were on the spot, that I feel particularly reluctant to offer a plan for a work to be erected at so great a distance.

But should even my plan be adopted, the sum of 350 Dollars (which is the reward offered by the S. Carolina Trustees) is a very inadequate reward only for the labor it would cost me, deducting the actual expense of my office. For before the fair & decissive drawings can leave the office a voluminous map of drawings of the whole detail must be made, first in the rough, and then in two fair copies, one for myself, the other for my employer.

In one late instance, however, similar to the present the flattering request of a Gentleman high in the public, as well as in my private respect has induced me to give a design for the City hall in New York. I have done so under the express stipulation, that I shall not be considered as a Candidate, if even my design shall be preferred, unless I have the sole direction of the work, appointing my own superintendant, and at the same time rendering myself fully responsible for the success of my plans, & for the conduct of the Superintendant. On these terms I have executed the two great works which have been committed to my care here. They have secured to the public a consistency, an uniformity & a promptness of operation, which cannot be expected from the measures of any Committee; & to myself, the satisfaction of perfect success.

After taking up so much of your time, for which I hope you will pardon me, I beg leave to say, that I will send to *you* a design for the S. Carolina College; not laboriously elaborated, but fairly sketched, & leave it to you to do with it as you please, provided, if it should be thought worthy of preference, I shall be permitted to send a person to superintend the work. I will then send also the detailed drawings & instructions, & if possible visit the spot myself once, which will be sufficient. As to compensation, there will be no difficulty in arranging it with me. I shall be very *easy* on the subject, if the terms of contract over the erection are liberal, & I can assure myself, that my character will not, (as it does most disgracefully at Richmond in Virginia) depend upon the *improvements* & embellishments of another. I must however solicit, that you will please to inform me what number of Professors & Students it is intended to accomodate in the house, & whether Stone or Brick is to be employed. Great accuracy is not required; your ideas, if you have not perfect information, will be sufficient.

I hardly know how to apologize for having taken up so much of your time & patience in answering your polite letter. I beg you will however consider my readiness to transmit to you a design, as it sincerely is intended, as a proof of my wish to prove to you how respectfully I am,

Your obliged faithful hble. Servt.,
B. Henry Latrobe.

The many marks of haste in the above arise from my wish to answer by return of post, & I must beg you to excuse them.

Selected Bibliography

BOOKS

Anonymous. *Acts of the General Assembly of the State of South Carolina.* Columbia: D. & J. J. Faust, 1808.

Cooper, T., and D. J. McCord, eds. *The Statutes at Large of South Carolina, 1682–1838.* 10 vols. Columbia: A. S. Johnson, 1838–1841.

Drayton, John. *A View of South Carolina as Respects Her Natural and Civil Concerns.* Charleston: W. P. Young, 1802.

———. *Letters Written During a Tour through the Northern and Eastern States of America.* Charleston: Harrison and Bowen, 1794.

Gallagher, Helen M. P. *Robert Mills, Architect of the Washington Monument, 1781–1855.* New York: Columbia University Press, 1935.

Green, Edwin L. *A History of Richland County.* Columbia: R. L. Bryan, 1932.

———. *A History of the University of South Carolina.* Columbia: The State, 1916.

Hamlin, Talbot. *Benjamin Henry Latrobe.* New York: Oxford University Press, 1955.

Hennig, Helen K., ed. *Columbia, Capital City of South Carolina, 1786–1936.* Columbia: R. L. Bryan, 1936.

Hollis, Daniel W. *The University of South Carolina.* Columbia: University of South Carolina Press, 1951.

Hooker, Edward. *Diary of Edward Hooker, 1805–1808.* Washington: Government Printing Office, 1897.

LaBorde, Maximilian. *History of the South Carolina College.* Columbia: Peter B. Glass, 1859.

Michaux, F. A. *Travels to the West of the Alleghany Mountains, in the States of Ohio, Kentucky, and Tennessea, and Back to Charleston, by the Upper Carolines.* London: D. N. Shury, 1805.

Olmsted, Frederick L. *A Journey in the Back Country in the Winter of 1853–1854.* New York: G. P. Putnam's, 1860.

Prime, Alfred Coxe, ed. *The Arts and Crafts in Philadelphia, Maryland and South Carolina, 1786–1800.* New York: Da Capo Press, 1969.

Ravenel, Beatrice St. J. *Architects of Charleston.* Charleston: Carolina Art Association, 1964.

Reps, John W. *The Making of Urban America, A History of City Planning in the United States.* Princeton: Princeton University Press, 1965.

Ruskin, John. *The Seven Lamps of Architecture.* London: George Allen, Sunnyside, Orpington, 1897.

Savage, Henry L., ed. *Nassau Hall, 1756–1956.* Princeton: Princeton University Press, 1956.

Sims, J. Marion. *The Story of My Life.* New York: D. Appleton, 1884.

PERIODICALS

Keith, Elmer D., and W. L. Warren. "Peter Banner, His Building Speculations in New Haven." *Old Time New England*, LIII (April–June, 1963), 102. Also see: XLV (April–June, 1955), 93–102; XLVII (October–December, 1956), 49–53; XLIX (April–June, 1959), 104–10; LVII (January–March, 1967), 57–76.

Mills, Robert. "Essay on Architectural Monuments." *The Analectic Magazine*, I, No. IV (April, 1820), 277–78.

Sizer, Theodore. "John Trumbull, Amateur Architect." *Journal of the Society of Architectural Historians*, VIII (July–December, 1949), 3.

Taylor, B. F. "Col. Thomas Taylor." *The South Carolina Historical and Genealogical Magazine*, XVII (October, 1926), 204–11.

Wilson, Charles G. "Robert Mills, Architect." *Bulletin of the University of South Carolina*, No. 77 (1919).

UNPUBLISHED MATERIALS

Bryan, John M. "Boston's Granite Architecture, C. 1810–1860." Unpublished Ph.D. dissertation, Boston University, 1972.

Carrot, Richard G. "The Egyptian Revival: Its Sources, Monuments, and Meaning (1808–1858)." Unpublished Ph.D. dissertation, Yale University, 1961.

Hall, Louise. "Artificer to Architect in America." Unpublished Ph.D. dissertation, Harvard University, 1954.

Manuscript minutes of the Board of Trustees of the South Carolina College, 1802–1865, South Caroliniana Library, University of South Carolina.

Manuscript minutes of the faculty of the South Carolina College, 1805–1862, South Caroliniana Library, University of South Carolina.

Manuscript records of the Clariosophic and Euphradian Societies. South Caroliniana Library, University of South Carolina.

Thomas S. Twiss Papers. Manuscripts, South Caroliniana Library, University of South Carolina.

Williams-Miller-Chesnut-Manning Papers. Manuscripts, South Caroliniana Library, University of South Carolina.

Index

The following terms are not indexed because they are directly or indirectly referred to on almost every page in this book: the South Carolina legislature, the South Carolina College (later the University of South Carolina), particular parts of the campus, the Board of Trustees as a body, the city of Columbia, and Richland County.